Love Always, Hobby and Jessie

A Memoir

Sara Robinson

Love Always,
Hobby and
Jessie

March 2010

Holly —
I'm so happy to U-CONNECT
with you!
I hope you enjoy this.
All the best,
Sara

PathBinder Publishing, LLC
Cover Design: PathBinder Publishing
Cover Image: Hobby Robinson's Collection

Carolyn

"In the atoms that bind us lie truths that only powerful forces can liberate, and such is the power of love."

Sara's creative and colorful writing style incorporates the use of metaphors to give the story a new dimension and additional depth. Stimulating all the senses, Sara's writing creates images in the reader's mind that play like a movie reel. The textures and details invoked by the combination of all these attributes will place the reader right in the story, setting and plot.
- Steven Knight, Premium Promotional Services

The author presents many moving vignettes of her parents, both sad and humorous. The story of the slowly decaying head of a trophy fish (mounted by an undertaker rather than a taxidermist) achieves a "scratch and sniff" level of vividness. Thanks to Hobby's pictures, everything (including the fish) is illustrated, and the book concludes with some of his best pictures of the people of Elkton. The memoir is itself a kind of photographic portrait. The photographer recedes into the background, and the "love always" of the title is expressed in a tender but honest portrayal of her parents.
- Brantly Womack, Washington, D.C.

Sara Robinson's engaging memoir is proof that the simple acts of living and loving make monumental ripples through the passage of time and deserve their immortalization in ink.
- Rose Red, Ohio

This book is a great read, whether one grew up in a small or a large town.
- Linda Hood, Washington

The collection of childhood memories and stories, wonderfully told, is entertaining, easy to relate to and span a kaleidoscope of human situations and emotions.
- Maria Nargiello, New Jersey

It is a remarkable story about two people who spent years trying to make a go of their marriage and in the end, they reached a peaceful relationship.
- Elwood Parker, Florida

This is a story of love, love gone bad, and love finding itself again in a familiar comfort of old age needs. I LOVED this book!
- Cynthia Elkey

Table of Contents

Foreword..ix
Preface...xiii
Acknowledgements..xix

Hobby 1
Jessie 14
The Mystery of the Orbits...26
Those Were Some Legs 37
Hobby's Big Fish, The World Record 46
The Last Big Night at Sun Valley, VA 56
Drawer B 68
The Yellow Convertible 74
Ernie Can't Play Poker 91
The Black Hawk Waltz...104
Hattie Mae 111
Repairing Irons...118
Clean Kill...126
Brenda Lee Saved Christmas in Elkton 133
The Old Home Place 142
The Little House on Spotswood 151
Love Always, Hobby and Jessie 158
Scenes from Where He is Resting Now:
Images from Hobby's Photography Collection.............169
Author Bio 186

<<< *Foreword* >>>

Bonnie Gardner Shifflett

The Foreword is simply what the word implies. It is a preface, an introduction, a prefatory statement preceding the text of the book by the author or another person dealing with its scope of what follows.

When I was approached by the author, Sara Maude Robinson, to write the foreword for her book, "Love Always, Hobby and Jessie," I experienced three distinct emotions: humility to be considered; anticipation in attempting it; and doubt of my ability.

This foreword has not as its purpose to reveal the contents, but only to introduce the desire to pursue and peruse it for yourself. As you begin to read "Love Always, Hobby and Jessie," may I suggest you keep your eyes on the pages; your mind on the story; and your heart on the people to fully understand and appreciate the purpose to its conclusion.

It is not meant to be a biography or an autobiography, but a clarification of these people's lives from the inside by the only one who knows it. The emotions are revealed with no attempt to disguise or to secret the reality. The pictures will emerge, not only in the photographs that remain, but also in the words of the present from the past.

You will learn to know Hobby and Jessie best by their unique daughter and author of this book, Sara Maude Robinson. She is a unique blending of her heritage, her background, and her make-up forming her individual character, personality, and psyche.

The insights herein expressed reveal a family of artists who each exhibited the skills and qualities of their form of the fine arts. Read the treasure and savor the pleasure.

I will include one personal incident that remains in my memory and will ever. It was a cold, blustery afternoon, February 24, 1993 in the Elk Run Cemetery at the grave sites of Hobby and Jessie in their beloved Elkton. After the funeral service for Hobby Robinson by Rabbi Jonathan Biatch, he invited those gathered to join in their Jewish custom of filling the grave. A shovel was provided, but I took up a handful of the freshly turned earth and sifted it through my fingers. It was my personal goodbye to Hobby. After moving away a few steps to stand alone the Rabbi joined me with an offer of his handkerchief. I refused it, as I had the shovel, saying: "No thank you, this is Hobby and he will remain with me for a long time."

And he has, and I know many share this sentiment. Dedicated to Sara Maude Robinson:

A Secret Dream
If in your heart there's a secret dream,
No matter how foolish it may seem---
If it brings you the slightest pleasure,
It is to you life's richest treasure.
It may not bring you fortune or fame
Or make anyone recall your name---
It may seem to all a waste of time,
And may not make you a measly dime.
But, if it gives you a peace of mind
And helps you to break the toilsome grind---
If it's what you really want to do
And you feel that it's God's plan for you
Then, don't let go of your secret dream,
No matter how foolish it may seem.

-Bonnie Gardner Shifflett

<<< Preface >>>

"Just Being Happy is a Fine Thing to Do." Jessie, 1928

When I decided years ago that I wanted to write a story about my parents, I struggled with just what kind of story I wanted to tell. At first I thought, perhaps a novel, filled with interesting characters, fictionalized, facing challenging dilemmas, battling unknown forces, and all the other usual components that make a compelling story. But the more I thought about it, the more I was convinced that what I really wanted to write was a story about stories. My parents' real stories were better than anything I could dream up; and for what I couldn't recite as total fact, I could use my imagination to fill in the gaps or add some detail, all in the interest of telling a good story.

Here you have it. I have taken many liberties with the genres of creative non-fiction and memoir to provide stories about my parents, Hobby and Jessie Robinson. I relied heavily on the collections of my father's photographs and the books that he published. I needed both to launch my imagination and recollections. Their stories could mirror stories of many people anywhere, just like the photographic journals that my dad published about Elkton, Virginia mirrored the people and events of lots of small towns in the USA. Giving their stories a voice using written narration helped me create a memoir that allowed me to give something back to their memory. I wanted to give equal voice to both, but the stories may come across as heavily weighted toward Hobby. In those the reader will have to look closely to see the revelations of Jessie. My intent was to describe the dynamics between the two of them, and by extension some of the dynamics between them and me. The stories will show the low, high, and riptides of their lives. As I wandered into view from time to time, I struggled with how best to narrate their stories; and sometimes I had to do it as a true narrator, calling them by their names. In some cases, I called them Mom and Dad.

There are two inanimate elements of this book that can't speak, but in their very existence, captured and held all that was precious to my parents and to those who knew them in one way or another. These were the Graflex Speed Graphic camera that was Dad's true best friend, and Robinson's Department Store, which was the true family home.

That camera was the key to the friendly capture of anyone or anything that happened to cross in front of the lens. With every picture he took, at that moment, the object was forever held. Whatever a person was thinking or doing, when he or she was transported from the real world, in one blink of a shutter, he or she would never be the same. Dad created a unique time machine that allowed for that person to be forever held in that one special moment.

When I want to remember someone from my past in Elkton, I look first in Dad's books. When others have contacted me in search of someone, they ask if by chance that person might have been in one of Dad's books. Dad used his imagination and creativity to pose the person in just the right way, or set up just the right background. From this initial stage, he would shoot the picture, process the film, and develop and print the image onto photographic paper. He may have chosen several views from which to select just the right one to keep.

The only immortality that can ever be offered is what the camera and its film can render to paper. As long as the paper lasts, the subject is immortal. That is the power of photography.

The family store, which started as Miller's, through marriage morphed into Harry Robinson's Department Store, and ended its life as Robinson's Department Store, had a regal spot in the annals of local lore. This store, scene of many clips of life unfolding in the little town, with townsfolk entering its domain under the guise of buying trips, anchored the family to the very streets on which it rested. And in its rest, anchored the town itself.

One side street, an alley connected to the store, actually was renamed by the local town council after one of the most famous streets in the world, Ben Yehuda Road in

Jerusalem, Israel. This was hugely symbolic in the history of that store since it was Jewish by birthright. I remember some of the rural people, short on hard currency, bringing in items to trade for clothing and shoes. We received bushel baskets of sweet potatoes, green beans, packages of prepared wild game, and even a couple of Crosley cars.

Dad kept records on paper receipts, dated and filed in a special wooden bound book on the counter. He carefully valued what was offered to give the most credit toward a purchase. My parents and I spent a lot of time working in that store along with our clerks. Dad was the true marketer and salesman. He was motivated more by talking and selling than keeping track of what was sold. He was always the first one to greet a customer. Mom was the true operations officer. She kept track of monies in the cash register, paid most of the bills, recorded inventory, and promoted overall well being among us workers. As a toddler I played among and in all the counters and the merchandise. As I grew older I was primarily responsible for filling in, doing odd chores, sweeping up, wrapping packages, re-stocking shelves, counting merchandise. When needed I waited on customers and ran errands. I learned to operate the old floor model NCR cash register before I learned to drive a car. Working and living side-by-side with those who graced our store by their presence was the best compliment we ever received.

Maybe there were other important things that I have missed. There are some things I have not missed: No one knew my dad like he himself did. No one understood my dad like my mom did. What my mom did not know or understand about herself, was learned by my dad when she learned it, too. Mom believed in the individual's inherent ability to survive. She practiced this religiously and through this practice she found her own sense of happiness.

From the unusual payment of a car to the subtle scent of a fragrance, the conflicts, resolutions, and personalities of my parents unfold for the reader. How their individual profiles merged and parted and merged again is told from different views, all serving to present their improbable bond.

Mom was to Dad, as film was to his camera. Neither could carry on without the other. Their discovery process might have been too long for some, but for them, it wasn't long enough. And what was theirs early on came back so close to the end that they crammed in all that they could during the very short time left.

We all look, I believe, in our own way, in our own time, for redemption. Fulfilling a promise is redemption. I promised myself that I would write a book about the early years of my parents' marriage and with that promise I hope that I have given them something back in some way. While they may never know that I have done this, the book will be the time machine that brings them back to life during the moments that the book is read or the pictures are observed by anyone.

The unique attribute of paper, produced from living plants, is that in their death, the plants create a way to extend life—by the paper's very ability to carry an impression. Photographic paper, paper receipts from the store, paper in a book. It is all the same.

One life cycles to another life and then another life and on it goes....then somewhere at sometime someone inserts a little simple device to capture just one instant thing...

Sara

<<< *Acknowledgements* >>>

While I believe that it has just about taken a town and state to help me produce and release this book, I must thank as best I can those who have been the steel cord backbone of this endeavor. I don't want to leave out anyone who may have contributed in some way to the creation of this book. But if I have missed you, then I sincerely apologize.

I have told many of the chapters as stories through the years and I am grateful to my friends, family, and relatives who always seemed to like them and wanted to hear more. I have gladly accepted the patience, laughter, support, hugs, tears, and pats on the back from my Baton Rouge extended family; my Elkton(and Newtown) family; my Luray family; my Charlottesville chosen family (including Batesville, Gordonsville, Palmyra, Howardsville, Swope); my Corpus Christi chosen family; my special Dallas family—Meggen and David; and my special Huntsville family—Patrick, Paige, and Deanna.

I thank our long time family friend, Bonnie Gardner Shifflett who with such style and grace, accepted my request to write the Foreword. She has written many columns and poems about Hobby Robinson, and her love of our family is boundless.

My childhood friends have contributed more than they know and I hope that Linda, Betty Jane, Jo, Cynthia, Judy, Janice, Larry, Kenny, Hilda, Betty, Louise, Rupee, and many others know how much I appreciate them and cherish the memories.

I send a special thanks to my hometown friend, Erin, who gladly took on the role of marketing and promoting my book to her famous friends.

My neighbors and friends here in Charlottesville have impacted me in wonderful ways. The support from the Rover's Recess gang in reading some of the early drafts has been remarkable. They flattered me by insisting that I give them more.

I thank my friends at Recording for the Blind and Dyslexic, who, before my book was even in first draft,, volunteered to host a signing party; a true testimony of friendship.

A special thanks goes to Carol Landy who work-shopped some of the early chapters with me; and to Mary and Karen who listened to chapters, read my dad's books, and asked for more.

A special thanks goes out to Maria Nargiello for reading some of the early drafts and asking for more.

Thanks to Karen Marie Smith for the artwork for The Yellow Convertible and the Elkton map.

A thanks goes out to Nita E. Cole who inspired my father to keep taking pictures and creating books. By extension and with her friendship she helped inspire me to write their story.

Acknowledgments

My thanks and gratitude go to Heather Hummel, my agent and publisher. If not for her workshop, her editing, and her encouragement, I would not have been able to pull this all together into a printed work.

And, my partner of twenty-two years, Carolyn, has been the grounding force for the memoir. From the time she met my parents until now, she realized why I had to write this. She took on the challenge of reading the very first attempts, helped tend the verbiage with me, and listened as I talked. She pressed me to keep writing....

Hobby

To start with, let me tell you, he was simply handsome. Even the presence of considerable ears didn't overwhelm the natural, Eastern European carved facial features. Perhaps at nineteen a little too skinny, but never mind, he was good looking. He knew how to dress well, too.

Whether that was his own instinctive style or influenced by the affluence of his parents, who would know, and it was of no concern. The clothes fit and suited the young man, a most dashing presence in a rural agrarian community situated in a narrow river valley in the western side of Virginia. It must have been a notable contrast amongst mule skinners, tanners, loggers and farmers.

By all accounts he was held in high esteem by his family, with doting parents and doting sisters. Spirited and affable, he played practical jokes and enjoyed those played on him as well. He had a strong sense of self, and a good sense of humor. He captured his youth, his emerging adulthood, and the rest of his life on film. While his given full name was Randolph Miller Robinson, his nickname, Hobby, described the one side of him for which, to many, he was known best—his photography; and for most Hobby was the only name they ever knew him by. Between when he started his lifelong avocation and when he died, he recorded his history as photo intertwined with the history of his beloved hometown.

He flirted with all aspects of his hometown, including some of the wild side. Not all of that part was preserved in his extensive photo record. It would be an impossible task to separate him from Elkton, except for those early years of his marriage when he was in the Navy and Elkton competed for his devotion to his country and to his new wife. Later when his marriage started to come apart, he resorted more and more to his third love, escaping into a world that would ultimately reward him with an attention that he desperately needed.

Hobby lived life more between the ages of seventeen and nineteen than some people ever live. He managed to fit a little college in during those years, and only ended this when his family needed him back at home.

However, working some in the store did not detract from his attendance to his photography and to his emerging social skills.

Between his time of going on a high school trip and getting married only three years had elapsed. His courtship started when he was no more than twenty; and by twenty-one he was married to an attractive young divorcee named Jessie. That she was six years older than he was of no significance other than as fuel for various jokes of their relationship. It was amazing that he met her at all.

He had been born and raised in Elkton, Virginia and she had been born in a very small town just five miles away. However, as a baby Jessie moved to North Carolina with her family, resulting in no collision with Hobby until twenty-something years later. Relatives of Jessie had introduced her to him on one of her visits to the area—and so their story began.

He took many trips back and forth to North Carolina and in most cases he had a driving companion, Raymond ("Tuck") Tuckson. Hobby had mused in one of his books that the two of them must have made an interesting pair on the highway.

When Hobby and Jessie collided they didn't create a new world for anyone else but themselves. That this impact was historical has been documented quite well. That the life of the impact was rocked with turbulence, silence, flare-ups, more silence, resolution, complacency, withdrawal, denial, and finally acceptance was witnessed by few.

But there were the courtship and Navy days. If anyone had thought him handsome in civilian clothes, then the picture of Hobby would have been even greater improved by the sight of him in uniform. His flare for dressing in the 1930's and 40's style was not lost among the folds and flap

5

of a seaman's garb. He simply poured from one into the other, even to the way he wore his sailor's cap. The transition was seamless.

****

Now the Navy, that was when the best of their times came out and the photo record he created spoke for all of this. In that treasure trove of celluloid captivity, the permanence of what was "Hobby-in-love" was forever caught and was never released. As long as those pictures lasted, he would always have that time when he was happy, Jessie was happy, and no future was interfering with those very moments forever captured.

No amount of observation, no amount of these pictures being held, no amount of future contemplation of the two dimensional world of their existence, and no amount of imagination applied would ever enable one to look between the image and the paper to see if some clue as to what happened was somehow hidden. Even more fantastical there would be no magic to liberate anything hidden between image and paper to find a way to bring back the beginning magic between them. It was what it was and they were who they were.

When he was twenty-one years old, sitting on a porch, home on leave from basic training, looking for all the world as someone relieved to be on home turf, in quiet comfort, he would not have known, he could not have known, that his hobby would become his legacy. He was not thinking then of anything other than his young wife, their still young life together, and his hope that this time would pass quickly and he could go back home to his family.

The couple of years they spent in Melbourne, Florida bore the testimony of an idyllic life, filled with passion, filled with friends, filled with hope, filled with laughter…filled with the absence that anything could possibly go wrong.

Upon his discharge sometime in 1945, they returned back to Elkton only not to Robinson's. He decided to try out running a restaurant and playground, which he called "Hobby's Sun Valley." He ran this enterprise for about a year, and when it came to an auspicious end, he came back to Robinson's store full time. By this time, he was also a

father of a new-born girl and had turned his photographic attention to her as well as his beloved townspeople.

****

Hobby would have said, "I screwed up." But then he would have moved on. In his pact to keep some of his marriage, thus his life, together, he had to re-direct his energy to extending the other one thing he could do best — take pictures. He channeled all that was him into what was all around him — the local people.

The magnet was the store. Its integral part of the town served as the medium of attraction for gathering pictures, not just all the ones he took but also those he could collect. The store's strong magnetic force drew everyone in, and thus became the gallery of a great photographic collection. The store provided, too, the quiet place upstairs where his photography's darkroom became the cradle of his civilization. Everyone and everything was brought to life by his own mixture of chemicals and then laid to rest on organic matter, but in this rest lived again in conversations, laughter, tears, memories, and thoughts. No one else had ever undertaken such a task to document over three generations of people in a small town.

When he finally finished his life's obsession, Hobby had compiled over ten thousand negatives, perhaps over ten thousand photos, and published nine books—one counting for two editions. His last book, *Across the Alley*, was described as his autobiography. Certainly he revealed more about himself in that book than in any of the others.

Still we didn't fully know him, and perhaps that was the best mystery of all. He longed for the return of his youth for all the remaining half of his life. He needed so much to get back the confidence and surety that he gained from the Navy and his Melbourne time. He never felt that anyone totally understood why he took so many pictures and why he needed all the attention.

He could not grasp growing older and the possibility of being alone. For all the times he was convinced that he would precede Jessie in death, thereby solidifying in his mind his immortality by her living, he never anticipated her dying first. He got lost; even when he tried to look in his bathroom mirror and see himself at twenty-five, the best he could do was see himself as he really was, an old man, eyes no longer flashing, but giving way to dimming. His last attempts at finding love fell short of his own marks. He was not going to get back his swarthy looks or his famous charisma no matter what he tried. Finally he accepted that.

****

During a cold February, when he and I had the last conversation we would ever have, he was in the hospital. He had checked himself in, with complaints of gastric distress, and when he finally did call me, he had already been in the hospital for three days. He felt good that night, he said. And he sounded much like his old self when he mentioned over the phone that he was sure the night nurse really liked him. The doctors had solved his "little problem," and this attractive nurse had come in to tell him he could have anything he wanted for supper.

With his historical great charm, and bolstered by his belief that he looked quite handsome in his hospital gown, he smiled his best 1942 Navy broad beam. He did not know that the heart palpitations he felt were not from the mild flirtations he offered. He ordered the Lobster Thermidor.

The call came to me around 2 a.m. from a doctor on call. He wanted to know if anyone had called to tell me that my father was unconscious, the result of a cardiac arrest. No one had. The weather had deteriorated considerably in the Valley, making for treacherous driving. We agreed that I would leave Charlotte, North Carolina, where I was living at the time, at first light and make my way by car to the hospital. I arrived around lunch time and the fate of Hobby was now clear. He didn't recover and I had to terminate the life support.

To bid this man farewell, my father, this photography marvel, this chronicler of a townspeople, was tough. I could not appreciate his talents with the fullness he deserved. I doubt anyone could. But then no one could ever doubt that he loved his town. That was the one mistress he never gave up. Elkton was the true competition to Jessie. He captured every pose, every alluring event, and every detail of everyone that belonged to Elkton. In that sense, everything and everyone belonged to him. He was faithful to his craft and that was as personal as he got. He was faithful in his own way to Jessie. He could not leave her nor could he leave Elkton. Even his tombstone is inscribed, "Resting now in the place I loved most in life."

Jessie

Jessie Hazel Virginia Lough Overby Robinson. That's a long name by most standards. However, it was likely that very few people in or out of her life ever knew of the Virginia or the Overby part. Most likely very few, limited probably to less than ten, ever knew that Jessie had even been married before she married Hobby. That's the Overby part. It was such a brief marriage, around six months, that the inception and duration of the marriage went unnoticed by much of her immediate family.

The family found out via the preacher underground that Jessie and [no first name] Overby had run off and asked another preacher to marry them. This preacher, true to the rural honor code, sent word to Jessie's father, a preacher himself, that he was about the marry his daughter. A mysterious note is the only remnant of any record of the existence of Overby. Something he had written to Jessie may have foretold the doom that would later descend on their brief conjugation.

"You to your eyes are very wise, But not so kind. You in my mind are childlike-small-not wise at all, But dearer far than wise folk are and to my mind; you are that kind! I dare not hit you know, my picture of you. I let you think your cruelty makes me love you." -O—

If Jessie hadn't returned suddenly back to her home with details of this union having gone bad, her siblings would not have realized that Jessie's original planned escape wasn't the grand adventure she had hoped it would be.

****

Jessie had planned this escape for some time. Having met Overby while she was attending Louisburg College, she fell madly in love and in defiance of her parents continued to see him. Of all her siblings, Jessie was the most headstrong, at least of the girls. Her independent streak was peppered with a great deal of stubbornness; she viewed that one of her life's main purposes was to break out from the confines of her large family. From all appearances, it seemed that the family was solid and happy, although they struggled financially. They moved around a lot since Jessie's father was a circuit preacher. And this was after over thirty years as a school teacher. Wherever the family moved, one more addition could be expected. Jessie was born in Virginia and that might have accounted for her second middle name.

Jessie escaped the family by marrying someone against their will. Any hope of her living happily ever after was forever smashed when he struck her the first time. He drank. When he drank, he lost control of his temper, and Jessie must have been a convenient target. The last little thread of that bond was snapped when he shoved her onto a piece of furniture and her female area was damaged. How severe the injury was at the time, no one would know. But Jessie planned her second escape and this one returned her right back to her family. The divorce came quickly and Jessie never saw Overby again. Sometime later she learned that he had committed suicide.

A picture remains of Jessie from her college term with the inscription, "With All My Love, Jessie." To whom the picture was intended is anyone's guess, but a good guess would have been this was a gift to Overby. This may have been the picture referred to in the surviving note mentioned before. Somehow Jessie retrieved and saved this picture; it survived intact in its cardboard frame. She may have given it again, to Hobby, later when she met him; and then I, her daughter, found it years later.

****

Was it fashionable in 1929 to be divorcee? Certainly Jessie was attractive, even gorgeous by many standards. Lithe, slightly tomboyish-bordering on impish, her coal-tar, black hair was worn short and close to the head, ala Roaring Twenties style. She dressed very fashionably, which had been enabled by her working as a clerk in her home town of Rocky Mount, North Carolina.

Within the next few years she was introduced to a swarthy, handsome, well dressed, and charming young man. He, too, was a fashion plate, having gained his wardrobe and style from his father, a local clothing merchant in Elkton, Virginia. As the only son of a transplanted Jewish immigrant family, he was given all the

17

accoutrements that defined a new generation in a new country with all the opportunities ahead. Even the Great Depression was not felt as substantially here as it was in other parts of the country.

Somewhere in the timeline between 1929-1930 and 1937, Hobby and Jessie met, flirted, courted and married. From his home in Elkton, Hobby took many trips to North Carolina to meet her family. He struck up a friendship especially with one nephew who remained a lifelong friend.

Hobby and Jessie wrote back and forth between visits — letters that included photos. One memorable photo that Hobby sent Jessie was titled on the back, "How do you like the old homestead?" It was an aerial shot of his parents' stately brick home including, just behind it, the house that he and Jessie would be given as a wedding gift. This present would become their own Old Home Place. Other pictures showed them together dressed as if going to church or visiting. They looked sensational.

The subsequent marriage was his first, her second. He was twenty-one and she was twenty-seven. There was no doubt that the instant attraction was physical and the inevitability of marriage was foretold by their mutual desire. They married in North Carolina and this time her father officiated. The family adored Hobby and it was reciprocated.

On their wedding day, very close to Easter that year, one would not have found anyone happier than those two. They were the best dressed couple in the state. Jessie was in a light gray smart wool suit, with white neck scarf and white, wide-brimmed straw hat. On her lapel was a corsage and on her hands were starched-to-a-crisp white cotton gloves. Hobby was in a dark gray wool flannel double breasted suit, with dark gray shirt and white tie. He wore the trendy pork-pie for the wedding, and in future years and pictures, he either wore that pork-pie or a fedora hat. He seldom had his picture taken without the fedora.

They spent the first couple of nights of their honeymoon in downtown Richmond, Virginia; but this was just a stop on the main trip to New York City. From there they returned to Elkton where they began their housekeeping. This would be a brief stay, however, as Hobby had been drafted to the Navy. Soon, he was off to boot camp in Bainbridge, Maryland and from there he would go first to Pensacola, Florida for Naval Photography School then on to Melbourne, Florida for his final assignment. Jessie took

several trips to Bainbridge to see him and when he had leave, he came home.

Jessie joined him in Melbourne, and this was where the photographic story of Hobby began. His Naval school training opened up the whole world for him when it came to taking pictures. In his youth, his talents were confined to the limits of the small Brownie. But in the Navy he was exposed to the latest camera technology. He was introduced to the Graflex camera and this became his life-long camera of choice.

While his official Naval work was related to war time, his off-duty photography went right to his wife and friends. He experimented with black and white and hand colored photos. He tried color film and sepia media. He explored every way possible to take photos and from the amount of them, he delighted in taking photos of Jessie. She was his favorite subject.

The myriad of photos: In consideration of... In consequence of... Inconsolable... Multitudes of pictures. Multitudes of poses, together, separate, with friends, doing things, doing nothing. Alone. Together. Happy. Pensive. From every angle, of repose... of recline... prone... in the bath... at the clothesline... at the beach. All the Navy years... pictures and more pictures. The photos seemed endless.

For the consideration of being his wife, Jessie posed gleefully, somberly, beautifully. The consequences of these numerous captures of her life were permanent recordings,

photo documents, if you will, that for at least a part of her life, she was extraordinarily happy. The pictures didn't lie and they existed long after she was no longer there. She was once happy and content.

To have become inconsolable later when cracks appeared in the veneer of her was just another way to describe how her life took its major turn. It went from the halcyon days of their young adulthood to the darkest canyons whose bottoms could only be wars that erupted in the first decade and continued through the middle and later years of their marriage. All of this, before any peace settled in, would play out in the big and little dramas of Jessie that were foretold when she was in college.

In her notebook of written charms was the one statement, the one true thing that she knew, "Just being happy is a fine thing to do." That this happiness would not be easily gained, but lost and found over and over, was not foretold to her then. Robbed of happiness in a first marriage, finding it again in her second, losing it in that, but when?

She was not happy for years and years. She relinquished happiness for some unknown trade off that no one ever detected. Were Hobby's indiscretions really the cause of her lost happiness? It couldn't have been that simple. And it wasn't. When finally after all the many separations fell through, when she accepted that she and Hobby would live out their lives together, and that her fate was to remain with him, they managed to somehow figure out how to be happy.

They acted as if they were happy at the weekend VFW dances. They acted as if they were happy watching their own separate TV's at night. They acted as if they were happy at both of their 50th anniversary parties. They acted as if they were happy right up until she died. Sometime during all this time, the acting morphed into the real thing. Jessie collapsed at a friend's birthday party and never regained consciousness. He stayed with her all night at the hospital.

The final tribute to her acting was the incorporation of the college prophecy on her tombstone. That one true thing, just maybe was no longer about acting.

Just being happy was all that she needed to do.

The Mystery of the Orbits

When a man and a woman meet, and they are both very young, with some life experience, and the time is the 1930's, have they lived more then than most do in the 2000's? Did their commitments have longer lifetime implications than similar commitments made seventy-plus years later? Did the value proposition of marriage carry more value then? How did one learn that value?

Could it have been that only by living a life together, despite many odds, despite a war or two, despite a child, despite infidelity, and in spite of everything else in their lives, they may have figured out what they valued?

I witnessed many episodes of their confrontational marriage throughout my developing years — in the house, in the store, and in the town — as I watched my parents learn just what would eventually and ultimately describe their relationship.

My parents struggled greatly and sometimes grandly in their marriage. It wasn't without fireworks, or on the other extreme, large gulfs of silence. Early years of attraction fever gave way to a malaise that grew and grew through many years; and faced with the ultimate truth that they would spend their last years together they came to terms with each other. A truce was declared and it was not without its rules. But within the terms of this revised marriage contract they were able to get along and even enjoy each other's company from time to time.

****

As a youngster I sought some refuge in reading, and one of my favorite topics was astronomy.

I learned that we are all made of "star stuff."

Everything and everyone has a connection to the very beginnings of stellar life, the universe life.

When a planet orbits a star, the mutual gravitational pull creates the path that repeats itself throughout the courses of their lifetimes. In fact, the gravitational pull of other planets and bodies within the effective field of influence exerts enough gravitational pull that the affected planet's shape itself is molded under this same influence.

The surface of the planet can be modified by the impact of space objects that have come loose from an orbit and found their way into the atmosphere of the planet. If the errant object survives the test of the planet's atmosphere and is of some size, the consequences of the impact can be significant. A frequent occurrence in planet formation is that after impact from some stellar object, the planet itself may fracture and send adrift into space parts of itself to be forever trapped in a gravitational controlled path around it.

Stars proceed through youth, maturity and old age in a different life cycle from planets. Since stars are pure energy sources with constant chemical reactions, they can last eons or they can use up their fuel, burst into huge death throes exhibited by brilliance as layers of their bodies give way, then to end as a great dimness or a black hole from which nothing would ever escape.

****

29

My parents, just like everyone else, were made of star stuff. They both were planets, who thought each was a star; their battles mirrored the pulls and extreme heat generated by strong gravitational forces on each other. Both bodies battled for the prime position. These same forces would have been influenced by their own orbiting parents, the orbiting town, the orbiting siblings, the orbiting friends, the orbiting satellite that was their daughter, and a whole array of flotsam and jetsam that worked its way into the individual spheres of influence.

When they were young, in lust and in love, their mutual attraction was strong, fiery and unrelenting. They orbited around each other so tightly that nothing could have broken that hold.

They were happy, compatible, adventurous, fearless, and doomed. They had little in common after the basic conjugal joys and relationship chores were done. But when they figured this out, they were with child, and this had set them up for realignment.

One of them had to give way to the stronger influence of the other, and in this case, per the trend, Mom gave way to Dad. He was large in his life and with the reputation as an heir to a successful local retail merchant, and a budding professional photographer in his own right, Mom could not compete. Her extroverted personality and quick sense of humor appreciated in their Navy days in Florida did not hold the same appeal when they returned to their small town.

Besides that she didn't feel much like entertaining when she was pregnant. Pregnancy was difficult for her, and after multiple miscues, this last time (they agreed) had better make it all the way. She had a right then to be grumpy. All around, her siblings had started their families with not much trouble, but she wasn't so lucky.

She accepted her fate, and as she used to say during their famous card games back in Florida, "A card laid, is a card played." She would get through this, and once she had her baby, she could take a good look at her life and what she wanted to do.

She had the baby, a girl, and I turned out to be more work than Mom and Dad, for that matter, bargained for.

Their little universe had dramatically expanded; and now Mom and Dad had a little satellite in orbit. They had to nurture me, and discuss future plans for me; and this took precedent over most any other plans. Hobby saw this as a great opportunity to increase his photographic skills. At every turn, camera at his side, he didn't miss a move, a burp, a laugh, a drool, or a tantrum. He took many pictures of Jessie and me as a baby. She hadn't allowed him to get any pictures while she was pregnant, but a photo of the child right after the birth was fine. There were pictures of Mom and me, the little girl with black curly hair, plump body and quick laugh. Lots of pictures were taken, lots. I was now an extension of their marriage, a third party, and all their emotional investment in each other was on hold. Except that Dad had just one small flaw.

****

Dad couldn't help himself, he loved women. He gravitated to them. He pictured himself as the ultimate perfect mate and that every woman he saw in a troubled marriage (at least from his viewpoint) could be relieved of her angst by his attentions. He tried to hide this part of himself from his wife, family and friends. A few knew of his transgressions and somehow secret pacts were forged not to reveal any of this.

While the main protected target was me, Dad believed with all his heart that most people did not know about Marge, Ginnie (a waitress at Belle Meade Restaurant), and

33

a couple of others. Marge was the first and lasted the longest, some twenty-plus years. She lived over Verbena Tavern and worked at a sewing factory. I even worked for her two summers at the factory, oblivious to her relationship with Dad.

The waitress was another story, and this one was amusing in a doomed kind of way. For many months, Mom, Dad, and I would go to Belle Meade for Sunday buffet lunch. He always wanted to sit in a particular booth and would request this particular waitress. Dad had come to know her better since he also had been coming up to Belle Meade for weekday lunches. The irony here was that Ginnie knew more about Dad than he knew about her. When she showed up one day at the store with her five young kids in tow, somehow Sunday lunches were changed to the Elkton Restaurant. The excuse given was that Belle Meade had gotten too expensive.

Other women took their emotional toll on him as well, and in his last years when he realized that the changing things around him were not really changing for him at all, he took inventory, cut his losses, and made peace with Mom. She accepted the fact that she was not going to live anywhere else but Elkton. To live with me was not an option, too much had happened, too much distance, too much geography, just too much.

Mom and Dad decided how the household would be divided. She had agreed to do the linens and dishes. He had to do his own personal laundry and grocery shop for his own food. They agreed that they would live together as friends, each could do as he or she pleased; and the town would continue to believe that they were husband and wife. In solving one discord, they found harmony in another outlet, dancing. They got to be quite the dance couple at the VFW dances.

****

Dad was the tragic hero of the photograph and his expressions of emotion were conveyed via the eye of the camera lens. He captured everyone he could on film and into his books. He had a special ability to capture just the right shot of someone. He could pose them well and he could complete the picture with phrases that told entire stories in a line or two. What he could not say in life, he said in pictures, and this was just enough. His collection of pictures was huge and his storage of anecdotes and descriptions of all that he had captured was limitless. Even as words would fail him in his marriage, he had taken and still had lots of pictures of Mom. He kept every one of them.

****

At the end of a star's life, its mass increases many times and exterior layers of particles are shed into space, all before it gives out to blackness. Some close-by planets get swallowed up in the great swell and some just manage to get slightly tinged. Some get caught in an orbital tug of war that continues for infinity. Remnants of stellar expansion remain in their orbits, even though they are changed.

The books of photography, like the planets, remain in their own orbits, viewed from time to time by those who observe and study them in attempts to understand the creator. Some of the books get jettisoned when owners die, leaving them to be sold or given away. Some of the books remain in collections and are seldom seen.

The star that was Hobby has remained in his own orbit, and his wife, Jessie, has remained as the orbiting planet. Long ago spun off from the local group, I have been on my own elliptical course through the universe, a comet of sorts who has passed by the star and orbiting planets from time to time. Not yet bound, but not yet free.

Those Were Some Legs

On this particular morning, she could tell right away that the riptide had not appeared as predicted. She knew this because as she swam just past the second sand bar nothing tugged on her legs. She knew her legs were strong; and she believed her legs were her best attribute. On this day, their strength was not tested. Her strokes were smooth, and her legs and feet barely broke the water. As she raised her arms over her head the broken parted water slid its retreat back down along her side.

She loved the feel of the salt water on her face and when she looked up and took a breath, she could make out the shore, solid and still as she glided by. She was proud of her athleticism; she had always loved to swim and to run. She was a confident swimmer and knew no fear of the water. Her favorite stroke was the freestyle, but she liked the backstroke, too. Sometimes she turned over onto her back, just in the hope that she might see one of the jets come up from the base. She thought that one of them could have Hobby on board taking pictures of the offshore just where underwater shoreline drops off to the deep basin, some ten miles or so out. Hobby would be scouring for German U-boats that had been sighted.

The water was tepid, just like it had been for the past two months since she had arrived in Melbourne. She looked forward to her morning swims. The feel of the surf against her arms, chest and legs invigorated and soothed her. How she loved the water. During her morning swims she planned out her days. There was nothing to distract her and she could disappear into her thoughts without disappearing altogether. Most of her thoughts revolved around Hobby. When he got assigned to Melbourne, they both thought this was great. They had already been apart for months since they had gotten married, and that too seemed like forever. She had missed him and she knew he had missed her. They had caught up on all that they had missed in the mandated separation; now they made plans for the future. He had about another two years left to complete his service and then they could go anywhere they wanted. What he wanted, and she guessed she wanted, too, was to return back to their home in Elkton.

****

As he left that morning for his duty shift, Hobby thought of his wife who had just joined him. He found himself laughing at some private joke they had shared last night; he was tickled at the joke he had played on Jessie earlier that week. He had surprised her by coming home for lunch, taking a snapshot of her hanging out the laundry.

What had him amused was that he had caught her hanging up his shorts in a neat row on the clothesline. Only the two of them could have appreciated her "peeved" expression as he caught her with the last short pinned, button fly open. What he didn't tell her that day was that he had appreciated and admired her slender legs caught in that photo.

From the very beginning of their courtship, Hobby paid close attention to the physical features of his now wife. He loved her smile, especially since it seemed challenging at times to get one from her. She had a great sense of humor with a big laugh, but chose what amused her with care. She seemed to hold some things back.

She was very athletic for someone so slender and willowy. Many had been fooled by her hidden strength, including him. He learned early on that she loved the outdoors with a passion for swimming and running. Even though she only competed with her brothers and friends, she seldom lost a race, on land or in the water. Most of the women he knew were not outdoors types, much less with any physical ability of note. Jessie was very attractive to him and everyone else was easily charmed by her manners and good looks.

Hobby loved to fish and Jessie would join him often for surf fishing in the evenings when he got home. While he could swim and was athletic in his own right, he preferred to fish, rather than splashing around in the water. He was content to cast his lines from shore while watching Jessie race against an invisible competitor out in the surf.

Hobby and Jessie and their Navy friends spent a lot of time at the beach. Most of the time they spread out blankets, pulled out ice chests filled with food and beer, and sat around telling jokes and sharing stories. Everyone loved to hear Jessie tell about growing up in North Carolina. Her quick laugh was infectious. The guys always had Navy stories to tell. Since it was wartime, most of the talk was about what was going on with the Germans. They tried not to talk too much about that, at the wives' request, but chose to confine themselves to base life talk. That was not as depressing or scary. No one wanted to face the prospect that a husband might have to ship over to the European front. Idle talk eased its way into conversations and no one pushed it away. It was important to keep the peace on all fronts.

****

On this morning as she swam up and down parallel to the shore, she set a faster pace than normal. She was working off a slight hangover and the faster she swam the more she was convinced that she could out swim the stubborn headache. Soon she would have to give up and come into shore as she needed to get back to their house. Some friends were coming over later, and she had let two of Hobby's buddies talk her into an evening of cards. *These guys never learn*, she thought. *One day they just might get tired of her taking their smokes and their money.*

On her way back to the house she would stop at the PX and get some beer and stuff for sandwiches. Hobby would get home about four-thirty, and he could help set up the porch for playing cards. She smiled with the thought that he was good for about a hand or two, then he would give up. He would say to them, "Y'all just go ahead and have fun, maybe I'll take some pictures of you playing."

****

The Navy times were the best of times for Hobby and Jessie; and, in their enthusiasm for each other, the spread of that happiness to their Navy friends was generous. Jessie enjoyed everyone there and the friendships were reciprocated. Years later Hobby recalled how much he loved Melbourne and how he had longed to go back there. His photography collection expanded during his Navy tour; most of the pictures that remain showcased his wife and their friends.

When he was in the Navy, Hobby had no idea that some years into the future he would publish photographic journals. For in the service, all his energy was divided between Navy work and Jessie. His pictures captured her at the picnics, at the beach, in their yard, posed together, set in humor, set in serious tone, and set in love—all of them. Many of those taken by Hobby showed Jessie with her smile and winsome good looks. He had a special stroke with the camera. He experimented with color photography and hand tinting, but his talent belonged to black and white. There he could highlight with shadow, and tease the lighting to show off textures from hair to clothing to skin. Jessie's lithe body was revealed and revered in every shot. And where he could, he didn't miss a chance to capture those legs.

****

His personal pictures and negatives numbered well over ten thousand pieces. His collection was enormous and his photography production and creativity resulted in nine books. All of that came in time; in every book the commentary with each picture gave a snapshot of each subject. In his last book, which he described as his autobiography, he included six pictures of Jessie. This book was the second of his productions that was dedicated to her. And in each subject's picture and within the words, there was a glimpse of Hobby, right down to the last picture in the book.

In one of the upper windows of the store, he displayed for many years a manikin's legs; and when caught on camera it was ironic that those legs showed up in his books. They certainly weren't Jessie's legs, just some artificial resin facsimiles that on occasion were adorned with hose or socks, or posed unclothed to gain the attention of passers-by or a photographer. There was no life implied by those faux legs; they didn't swim anywhere, and they didn't run anywhere. If they were meant to be a reminder of something from the past, few knew. What they signified, other than Hobby's sense of humor, was anyone's guess.

But, if one had seen Jessie's legs back in the Navy days, pushing water aside in a surf swim, or gracefully holding up a short sundress, one would have thought, "now those were some legs."

Hobby's Big Fish, The World Record

Whwhen I was a youngster, I often spent quiet afternoons in my dad's office, looking at his many books. Among my favorites were two books on fishing that I could never get enough of. My delight in these books was initiated by the story my father would tell me about the time he held the world record for the largest Channel Bass caught on the East Coast, specifically in the Chesapeake Bay. I was always reminded of this story because we had the head of that record mounted and hung on the wall in the back of the store. The fact that placed underneath of it was a bucket, which for years caught the slow dripping remains and preservatives of that gamey (no pun intended) denizen of the sea, did not diminish the intrigue for me of how that fish head came to be in the first place.

****

The Channel Bass, aka Redfish, aka Red Drum, Bar Bass, Bull Redfish, Poisson Rouge, Rating, Reef Bass, Saltwater Bass, Red Bass, Sea Bass, Red Horse, is a member of the croaker family. Its scientific name is <u>Sciaenops ocellatus</u>. But by whatever local name this fish goes, it is considered among many fishing experts as one of the great shallow water game fish in North America. Its coppery brown red coloration has created the moniker for it of "coppery warrior of the tides." While surf casting is a most common method of finding and hooking the Channel Bass, another method is casting from a small boat in shallow bay or offshore waters.

The Channel Bass is described as having grayish, iridescent silver sides which shade to a copperish red towards the back. As the fish grows larger it becomes red all over. A round black spot, about the size of a fifty-cent coin, is found above the tail on the caudal peduncle. The mouth curls downward and the snout is conical. Using its snout, the Channel Bass loves to nose and burrow in the sand for crustaceans and other live "goodies." When Drum actively herd and feed on bait fish, however, artificial lures such as tin squids, plugs, and spoons will draw immediate strikes. Because the mouths are considered sinewy, larger-than-usual hooks are required, meaning 6/0 and 8/0 sizes. These fish are of hefty weight as well, and large capacity casting reels with test line of twelve to fifteen pounds are needed to ensure a successful landing. For specimens less than twenty pounds, the food value is considered fair to excellent, with five pounds and less as excellent. So, for those caught above the food value minimum acceptance, the catch thrill must not be culinary, but must be for appreciation of sheer size.

A large Channel Bass can weigh a considerable amount, and the last world record weight came in at ninety-five pounds, set in 1978 near the Outer Banks. So back in 1940 while fishing during the middle of summer in a forty-foot cabin cruiser off the Delmarva Peninsula near Wachapreague, Hobby Robinson hooked what seemed to be a lost wreck from a previous war. He found himself in a mighty battle. Little did he know when he felt the first hard tug at the line that he had hooked a fish prized by sport fishermen for its remarkable strength and doggedness. Much later that day he had over sixty-six reasons to appreciate having landed this champion and breaker-up of tackle. In subsequent pictures taken of Hobby and the big fish, he didn't look the worse for wear after having battled that behemoth for over an hour and a half.

Many, many years later I relived that part of my father's life when I returned home to bury him and settle his affairs. The discovery of that fish artifact set in motion the movie reel memory of what must have been one of the highlights of my father's young years. I am not sure he had remembered what had been the fate of that fish head for years then as he lay dying, or if he had even given it a thought. But when I found that relic, I was compelled to think of it with a fondness that I might have missed had it not been for the one time that my father held the world record.

****

The fact that the girth of that fish brought onto shore was thirty-four inches created immediate attention as the crowd gathered at the dock. The news had been already

48

radioed in by the captain and that dimension was the first thing he reported. When the boat docked and the fish was hoisted up on the scale, the real big number then appeared: sixty-six pounds and twelve ounces.

And from the tip of its snout to the tail, it measured a lengthy fifty and one-half inches. The measurements were officially recorded, and Captain Parker helped Hobby fill out forms to register the fish in the 1940 George Ruppert Fishing Contest. Later that evening he typed up an affidavit, had it notarized, and then sent it all along with the registration. For his part, as he had conveyed this most energetically to Hobby and his fishing buddies, and anyone within earshot, Captain Parker was confident that this was the largest Channel Bass ever caught in the Chesapeake Bay. This was bound to be a new world record.

As it turned out for the lucky Hobby and pals, this Channel Bass was a world record, duly noted and recorded and published in not only the local papers, but also in the national paper, The Washington Post. And in this publication, a picture of Hobby with the fish was included.

****

In my mind's recorder on playback, with some editing and developing, I can picture the day of the big catch unfolding more-or-less like this:

My dad's sister, Margaret, was pinch hitting in the store, their own Robinson's Department Store, along with my mother. When Margaret and Dad's father was alive, he ran the store with two of his adult children assisted by a daughter-in-law who helped clerk. From time-to-time Margaret was happy to work some additional hours in the summer when Dad left early for fishing excursions. It was already late July and in the two years that Mom and Dad had worked in the store, this was the first time Dad had left for three days. He and two buddies, Carl his best friend, and G.K. his brother-in-law were down at the Eastern Shore having a great time fishing, relaxing, talking, and drinking. Mostly they talked and drank.

For two of those days, despite all the local predictions, nothing was biting out in the bay. As July 29 lazily made its appearance, the usual store day itself woke up to the prospect of some business. About the middle of the afternoon, the lazy mood within the store was abruptly halted by the intrusion of the loud ring of the store phone. Mom, startled by the ring, answered it, and listened with the phone about three feet from her ear. Even Margaret, on the other side of the blue jeans on her favorite store stool could just about make out what Dad said. One thing for sure she knew, he was excited about something. Mom couldn't get in a word to stop him so he could catch his breath — he was running on so.

As it turned out, when Mom recounted the phone call to Margaret, Dad had told her that he had caught this whopper of a fish and that they were hanging around the docks to have it measured, weighed and then certified as a world record. Mom also knew from their fishing days in Florida that just about nothing could hold Dad's attention more than a good caught fish. If this fish was everything he said, then it would be a miracle if he even made it back home the next day.

Later she would remember the conversation just about word-for-word and how he insisted that it wasn't just any fish, but one that no one else had ever seen in the bay. For sure it was the biggest one taken that season, he went on to explain, and the boat captain, Captain Parker, believed this Channel Bass would be close to a world record. Mom and Margaret agreed that this was certain to be one fish story that would be told over and over again. Behind her amusement of Dad's adventure, she wondered just what he would do with that fish when he brought it home.

Funny as it might seem, since I was not even an atom wandering around in space at the time, I could put myself right into the action of the events on board the boat. I could see Dad hook the fish and yell out to his companions that something huge had to be on his line and it was putting up a fight. With its weight and with Dad engaged with the rod and reel, it must have been a battle of wills as much as strength. For about an hour and a half this engagement lasted until the fish gave in. Probably this was about five minutes before Dad gave out! It took all four men to haul that trailer park of a fish into the boat.

As they motored back to shore across the calm surf, they headed toward the docks where the Virginia Department of Fisheries had its weigh station. The crowds had gathered, news having spread across all the short wave radios on land and sea, to greet the fishermen and their catch. Many photos were taken and certainly Dad made a dashing presentation as another of the great white hunters. All agreed that the fish was a terrific specimen of the species and whose measurements would hold for some time to come. Dad filled out entries for several sponsored fishing contests, and later learned that he had won first prize in all of them. He took in about three hundred dollars in prize money, a small fortune in 1940 to him; and he received lots of recognition in sports pages and sports magazines. This was the highlight of his life.

I could further imagine what the next round of conversations would have been like regarding what to do next with that fish. Certainly it was well known that Redfish this size were not considered edible, so to save for future consumption would have been out. Fish spoiled pretty quickly so any decision as to its future would have been made fast. Taxidermy was not a consideration for this fish, for as far as Dad and friends knew only fur-bearing mammals and birds were known to be mounted in their home area. There was no doubt that this fish had to be preserved for posterity in some fashion.

Likely later that day an idea was fashioned from a conversation fueled by much beer and tale telling. Carl, the local undertaker in their home town, presented the idea to embalm at least the head. In his mind, I'm sure, there was no reason why this wouldn't work. The head would then be preserved, just like in ancient Egyptian times, mounted on a large plaque and hung up somewhere. It wasn't hard for them to imagine such a grand fish, with its soon-to-be-even-grander head on its own, infused with formaldehyde, nailed to a shellacked board of sturdy oak, and hung regally placed on a special wall. Carl would work his magic and there the fish would be, a record memorialized.

****

Where the fish head hung while Dad was in the Navy is anybody's guess, but probably it hung in Robinson's store. It made the trek to Sun Valley for a short while and then returned to the store where it was relegated to the back

53

over the door leading to the loading dock and storage area. What glory that might have remained was shared with the blue jeans and work jackets. Regrettably, that fish head had become demoted in historical importance. The major contribution to its fall from fame was really due to its own undoing, literally. For as it turned out, that embalmed head started dripping some vile fluid about six months after it had been hung in its hall of fame location. Despite the stories, despite the offered autographs, despite the pictures, no one wanted to linger near that fish with the awful bucket underneath, catching what might have been its dissolved innards. During this deterioration, the fish head was slowly losing its identity to where later it was darn tough to even recognize it as a fish head at all.

****

As my father aged, and after my mom had died, he sold the store and all its contents. He must have forgotten about that fish head; and no one else was around to remember that historical day some fifty years prior, when Dad caught that fish. The new owners of the store had packed up some remains of the store and put them aside to deliver to him later. All of these were forgotten as well, until I returned home to bury my father. As I cleaned out his little storefront business, Hobby's Photo Memories, I was presented with the other boxes. I happened upon one box and it contained the forgotten fish head, left in its state of suspended reputation.

As much as I had hated parting with that fish head, having taken it unceremoniously to the dump, I realized that what had been important was the significance of the day my father had caught the grand fish and how its presence was a reminder to him and anyone else who happened to see it that anything was possible. During my childhood, I had not minded the bucket underneath the fish. I liked looking at that head, and even in my later years, I still thumbed through the scrapbook made by my mother of all the articles about my father catching that grand fish.

What I visualize is the big bay on a summer day, gently rolling swells, and lots of blue sky. What I imagine is a large Redfish, or Red Drum, or Coppery Warrior looking for food or interested in something shiny ahead of it. The picture I construct is this bold young fisherman anticipating a big catch, eyes moving back and forth between the casted-out line and the horizon. He listens, he looks for some small sign of interest in the water. Not a sound comes from the boat. It is just him, waiting, lure doing its job and hook at the ready.

What I smell is the salt air.

The Last Big Night at Sun Valley, VA

The yellow card that fell out from behind some old papers had written on it, "Hobby's Sun Valley, 'Playground of Virginia.' Elkton, Virginia." On the bottom of the card were listed: "tavern, tennis, dancing, swimming, riding, and hiking." If one wanted to make reservations or to speak to the owner, Hobby Robinson, all one had to do was ask the operator to ring 1-F-4. I found the card as I was looking through some old photographs and papers that I had filed away after Hobby died. The tavern itself abruptly closed when I entered Hobby's life, but for a brief time, it was a place of repute, in a manner of speaking.

****

In the late 1940's for about a year or so, it was the hotspot of the area, known for its food and its rollicking good times. Would anyone have predicted that this cute little tavern would give a new definition to good times? Before Hobby bought Sun Valley it was known as a local campground that offered swimming, hiking, tennis, etc. When Hobby took over, the main building was converted to a restaurant and Sun Valley started out as a supper club where the local chemical company executives and businessmen took their wives out for dinner and dancing to a live band. These were the Elkton middle class with respectability, nice homes, nice cars, groomed yards, garden clubs, Lion's Club memberships, and either businesses to run or departments to manage. They would have a few cocktails, relax, talk some business, enjoy a nice cut of beef, and find out who had just bought a new car. Couples would seek their usual places with their regular friends; and the laughter and drinking were tempered by the offsetting reality of the resumption of their routine lives the next day back in town or at the plant. As one could predict, they didn't stay out too late either.

This typical night time setting didn't last too long and like a coral reef that finds itself losing its native species to an invasive new group, so did the transformation of the tavern imitate nature. But unlike a coral reef that might successfully balance the original residents with the new species taking residence, once the tavern clientele shifted to a less refined, raucous bunch, there was no balance of nature. The transition moved from townies to the good ol'boys and girls from the country.

The dark suited, neck-tied, ironed and starched, fancy appareled, dressed crowd gave way to the jeans, boots, cotton T-shirted, sleeveless bloused, heavy drinking, car racing and partying roadhouse types. They didn't care about a quiet evening with manners and all that. These folks were the wild and wooly part of the local area. Their addresses would have read more like roads with "Hollow" in the name, not "Avenue."

Elkton was notorious for its rough inhabitants living close to town; when they took over Sun Valley, the allure to those who wanted to walk a little on the wild side was confined to those who had already experienced it. The rest of the local society avoided the wild side. Hobby mixed easily between the two groups from his family's clothing store business. He had seen some of the wild side first hand with a few of his friends, but nothing serious had ever come of it. His parents had been loving, somewhat indulgent, but persistent in their firm appliance of discipline. They wanted Hobby to be a respected Jewish gentleman, long before he turned thirty.

For his own part, as Hobby saw the transformation, he was caught up in this allure of a rough crowd with their big drinking, big spending, and big talking. Hobby wanted to experience a little of his life on this edge. How did he get so emboldened having just mustered out of the Navy?

He wasn't in the armament part, nor was he a fighter pilot or a Navy Seal. He was a photographer. All his prior action was from a distance, safe. Did he have to see another side of life that somehow he thought he missed? While Hobby and Jessie had wonderful times in the Navy, now they had to take a hard look at what their lives would be in the future. Jessie wanted Hobby to settle down. By now he and Jessie had been married for almost ten years and his wife was pregnant, again. And this time, with all the proper bed rest, she might actually carry the baby to term. Jessie was determined to complete the pregnancy and she was firm that Sun Valley would not be a distraction.

****

So what made him think he could be a restaurateur? By his own admission, he told his sister before leaving the service, he wanted to loaf about and fool around with his photography. He didn't need money and he didn't want any extra responsibility. He didn't want to go back to the store either. He wasn't sure what his options were, except for his responsibility to his wife. He had saved enough money from the Navy to do about anything he wanted. When the tavern and its property became available, it proved too good to refuse. He also managed to buy the old truck with "Sun Valley, VA," painted on the driver's side.

****

He hung his prized possession, the embalmed head of a huge fish he had caught, from years prior, up on the wall behind the bar. Because it had been embalmed by his best friend, the local undertaker, instead of properly prepared by a taxidermist, the fish had a slight leaking problem. But no one could see the bucket below it behind the bar. He talked about his world record fish and the famous trip to "The Bay" where he caught it. He had framed his certificates and he could point to them whenever he needed to reinforce the facts. These were the glory days for fish, tavern, and Hobby.

Most work days for Hobby were spent getting in liquor, food and other supplies. He would plan out the evening's menu, talk with the staff, go home for lunch and visit with his wife. He didn't talk much about his photography then. While he took a few pictures, mostly of his friends and of the early customers at the tavern, for the most part his photography was on hold. It was odd though that of all the pictures taken and of those remaining in photo collections, there were no pictures of Jessie pregnant or of her at the tavern; and no pictures showed up of Hobby at the tavern. Just those couple of pictures of the early patrons and one picture taken outside of the tavern itself were kept. There is a picture of Jessie and Hobby's sister, Margaret, standing by another Sun Valley "car" parked in town. And, given the year of that picture, 1942, it was taken before Hobby actually owned Sun Valley.

****

If anyone took notes or names that documented all the events that took place in the latter days of the tavern these are long gone. There were no records, so anything that remained to recount the events was oral history and folklore. All that remained were memories of the liveliness of the place and stories about the bands, the drinking, and the fighting.

Every Saturday night, when the country music bands revved up, the usual crowds would not have missed the times there for anything. The more the bands cranked, the more the alcohol flowed. The louder the bands got, as they played to a fueled crowd with too much bravado to make any sense, the more tenuous the situation became. It was clear that a path toward an inevitable end, and not a good one at that, was in the brewing. Bodies teetered out of control and rapidly became the heavy equipment destined to level the place. These events continued through every Saturday night and built up the unstable caldron over a few years. Word spread throughout that part of the Shenandoah Valley that Hobby's was the "in place" for hot music, hot food, hot women, hot heads, and cold beer. Boiler makers were the standard fare and the addition of whiskey contributed more to the charged atmosphere destined to future destruction.

Since the pictures are in my head, I can visualize the events progressing like this: Yelling would have started inside, with the participants ushered outside to finish their business. The fights started as minor incidents. Hobby was able to control these minor flare-ups most of the time. Most everyone was handled without any show of force or without even the county police. Evidence of settlements was often seen by the next Saturday night on the fellows. Some bruises were worn like military medals, with the cuts and scrapes as badges of honor that took on heroic proportions when any of the women asked about their origin. Sometimes a woman's honor had to be protected or someone's girl had to be defended against unsolicited advances. The fights took the place of discussions. There was no gentle resolution of problems. There was no polite dialogue to soothe ruffled feathers or dissipate an insult. After drinking, no one talked about going for a swim or playing tennis. This crowd would not have appreciated the refined pleasures of the town classes. Their actual playground was always inside the tavern. Racquets were replaced by fists and scores were kept in heads intent on getting even.

When the tavern finally lost control, it had already been on a downward spiral toward its ultimate demise. As the Christmas season of 1946 went into full swing, wartime was over and the country lifted up economically. The general attitude was optimistic for the good times ahead. Money was available and people spent it again. And since the roadhouse was on a major north-south route through the Shenandoah Valley, it benefitted from some of that money as well. Bands got paid and they competed to play at Hobby's. Action was the name of the game, and the free spending and big drinking group was in place to create and receive all that was there.

On the fateful night of Christmas Eve 1946, Hobby had told Jessie he would be late. He expected a big crowd; and clean-up after closing would take longer than usual. He would stay so he could let his workers go home early in time for Christmas Day. Though she hadn't set foot in the tavern for months, she had heard about all that was going on there. Most of her information had not come from Hobby. She had heard plenty and she didn't like one bit of it. She knew all about the restaurant's rough crowd. She had heard that Hobby partied right along with the customers. She had heard about the parking lot fights over the women. She had heard lots of stories and gossip; yet she hadn't heard everything. Consequently, during this particular spell with the tavern, Jessie was not exactly on speaking terms with him, having chosen to say nothing when she couldn't think of anything good to say. When Hobby told her he would be late, she figured it was last minute Christmas celebrating; and, all she wanted was for the night to end peacefully, if not silently. Since she had given birth about two weeks previously, she was very concerned about the escalating activity at the tavern and Hobby's safety.

****

By about ten o'clock the fights started. Hobby hadn't heard what started the commotion. He'd just told the band to play his favorite song, "Divorce Me C.O.D.," and he was back behind the bar wailing out the words to that fish head as he mixed drinks and opened beer bottles.

His first clue that something was terribly wrong was when he saw an airborne gin bottle headed straight for him. It missed. When he stood back up, he saw that several couples started arguing with each other; then the next thing anyone knew, tables were overturned and chairs thrown. Bottles flew all over like hand grenades seeking foxholes. When they landed in loud shatters on the band's stage, the guys abandoned their instruments and took off out the side door. In all the confusion one of the band members tripped over the bass drum, but the sound of that collision was masked by the first of the gun shots. All hell broke loose. The hot air from shouting, from fists that separated smoke-filled air to connect to jaws, and from fired gunpowder turned the inside of the tavern into an enormous pressurized cooker ready to blow its lid off.

Bottles and heads were broken and chairs and tables were scattered everywhere; when the last of the noise and people were gone from the scene, the air cleared around Hobby. He sat on the floor, in the middle of the carnage, having salvaged one bottle of whisky intact. Beside him he found about twenty of his business cards that had fallen out of his pocket. He was pretty sure he hadn't been shot; and he didn't see any other bodies or parts around him either. He had a couple of scratches, but otherwise was unharmed.

What the hell, he thought, as he decided he might as well have a drink. He looked around and saw broken bottles, splintered chairs, and shattered glasses. He smiled a little when he saw that his trophy fish was still holding court over the bar. Some drunk had accurately lobbed his fedora on top of it. He raised the bottle in a salute to his grand fish as a personal toast to what he knew was the last night Sun Valley would be open. He finally got up and did the best he could to sweep up the place. The bar's counter was a wreck so he took the floor broom and just pushed it along the whole length of the bar top, bulldozing bottles, ashtrays, napkins, his own tavern trading cards, and cigarette butts into a barrel at the other end. The rest would have to wait until his help came back. The great adventure of tavern ownership came to its abrupt halt when it ended with a real, movie-style shoot-em-up.

After he got home, as the sun rose on that cold, cloudless, Christmas Day, Hobby told Jessie his roadhouse days were over. She smiled as she handed him their sleeping baby girl, brought him a couple of band-aids, and offered to fix him breakfast. She never said a word about how he reeked of smoke, fried something, and alcohol. She never said a word about Sun Valley nor did she ask him the source of the lipstick stain just below the collar of his shirt when she did the laundry a couple of days later. She decided he would never miss that shirt anyway.

Drawer B

By the time the last of the lights in back were turned off, I would have put down the last of the oiled sawdust. This red, pungent mixture would remain on the floors overnight to pick up any soil or other tracked in street residue. Whoever arrived first at the store the next morning would grab up the push broom and sweep up all the remains. This ritual repeated every time the store closed.

I loved the routine of applying the sawdust on those dark, hard floors. The contrast of the red against the floor was subtle, but I still liked the visual sensation it created. Something about the finality of the day within those colors solidified the end of the sun and the beginning of night, with the store left to rest. As we walked out the door, one last wisp of that oiled dust hitchhiked onto a shirt sleeve to accompany me to the car.

Most times the close was done by Dad with me to assist on occasion. Mom would have gone home several hours earlier to prepare dinner and attend to any housework that needed attention. While I finished the floors, Dad emptied the cash register and counted the day's receipts from each of the cash drawers. Everyone who worked at the store was assigned a specific drawer where his or her sales were put. Dad had drawer A, Mom had B, Ernie had C, and I shared D with the others, such as Anna Lee, Betty, Hilda, or Marian. Once he had everything counted he wrapped the bills and rolled the coins. He filled out his deposit slips and placed it all this into his bank bag. Then he took this back to his safe in the rear of the store for the next morning's trip to the bank. When I was real little, he let me play in the safe, where I put empty gun shells or buttons or coins in the various cubby holes. I loved the smell of the inside of that safe. It was of old iron, paper money, and waxed wood; and even as an advanced age adult, I have no trouble conjuring the memory of that smell.

Some things, like scents, just never leave you. Odors, fragrances, and aromas can speak volumes of life's workings, without a sound uttered. Of many enduring memories, the power of a remembered scent ranks near the top with its association to people, places, events, and life.

****

Such it was for me with scents. I could list all of the scents associated with the store: The oiled sawdust for the floor; the inside of the glass water container in the fridge beside the furnace; the inside of the safe; Dad's office — with its combination of Old Spice, store receipts and photographic supplies; the mustiness of the mounted animals placed all around the store; the crisp dark inky smell of denim jeans stacked up on counters; the scent of the rubber Arctic galoshes on the basement stairwell; the chemicals in Dad's darkroom; the wool hunting jackets hanging in the back of the store; the bucket beneath the aging fish trophy in the back; the inside of the men's hat boxes; the wool baseball caps; and, the stacks of cotton work socks. When customers or friends came to the store, the intrusion of their own scents did not offend. These temporary intrusions rapidly disappeared when their conveyances left, allowing for the store's own unique aromas to settle back in.

I could not associate any particular fragrances with any particular individuals, except for one. I always knew when my Mother entered the store, or any room for that matter. No one else I ever knew used Elizabeth Arden Orange Skin Cream; and for all of her life I associated that scent with no other. My mother's unique scent never left quickly. Whenever she and I had one of our fractious encounters, that orange cream would remain to remind me that I had lost the argument or battle, long after she had left the scene.

When I was a kid and first comprehended that she and my father no longer shared a bedroom, I heard them exchange good nights as I drifted off in my own world. I heard her footfalls as she retreated to her bedroom, with his entreaties to come to his room, spoken quietly and beseechingly, only to be diluted and dismissed by the power of a night cream as it propped its mistress's head on a crisp cotton pillowcase.

The last thing she would do at night before retiring would be the application of this cream. It kept her ageless many had said. Only her gray hair gave any hint as to what her actual age might have been. The skin on her face was smooth and not deeply marked or lined by troubles of marriage, child rearing, smoking, or life. Even though she was a heavy smoker, she defied all the connections between smoking and aging. She and her cream were stronger than anything tossed to her.

****

When my mother was in her late sixties, I took her with me to visit the Elizabeth Arden factory in Roanoke. The company was a customer of my employer and on previous visits I had told the purchasing agent of my Mother's fondness for the Orange Skin Cream. When he suggested that on my next visit, I bring her along, I was complimented. On the day that we stopped by, he surprised both of us with a large box of samples. After talking a bit, he presented this box to my mother; and as he slid it over his desk, he reached in and grabbed a large pink container. It was a one pound jar of Orange Skin Cream—the largest size made. With a grand show of chivalry, a courtly bow, he offered the jar to her, and said, "With my compliments."

She was speechless, almost. But she managed to return the gesture, bowed her head, eyes fixed on him; and, with a most gracious thanks, and a wink, assured him that this jar would last her the rest of her life. He beamed and returned to his seat. For years she never forgot him, and I had to wonder if he somehow associated the fragrance of that cream with her from then on.

****

The store is now long gone; my parents are now long gone. I have saved the old cash register which has remained with me all these years and now sets regally in a special bedroom in my own home. It keeps company with the bedroom suite that I was given by my dad that once belonged to his parents. (This mahogany suite has a unique scent of its own.) I have the side-by-side cabinet in the room as well, and in it I can still capture a remnant scent of shotgun shells and gun oil. Competing for scent attention are a wooden box containing some old silver dollars, a couple of Sun Valley trading cards, and some little ceramic dolls with crocheted dresses that belonged to my mother.

Many of the sensorial associations I connect with my parents are still around. Kept alive by memories, I can pull them out and enjoy them just about any time I want. The most pervasive one is the Elizabeth Arden Orange Skin Cream. Even though I put that jar in her casket with her when she died, I didn't lock away the scent.

Somehow, some way, every time I open Drawer B, I get just the faintest whiff of her, that scent of orange.

The Yellow Convertible

There were many battles between my parents, Hobby and Jessie, during my childhood. Some lasted days, some just minutes; some resolved themselves amicably, but some did not. And, some were resolved by payments that were meant to be reminders of the consequences of a particular transgression.

****

I'll always remember that car. And I can remember much of the day that I saw it for the first and last time. What a fantastic automobile it was, a bright canary yellow with black ragtop. It had about a million pounds of chrome on the front and back, and it simply looked magnificent parked right there, on the diagonal, in front of our store. The morning sunlight cast a huge glow all over the car, and even the chrome seemed to break up the sun into hundreds of little suns all beckoning the day to look at this incredible vision otherwise known as a 1948 DeSoto convertible coupe. The interior was black leather seats and carpet; and even the black steering wheel had miles of inlaid chrome and shiny metal. When I looked at the wheel, I could see me looking right back at myself, smiling with delight.

When I first saw the car, it had just been driven up to the space by my dad; and when he emerged I came running out of the store with unrestrained glee that this car might actually be ours. I remembered, too, that I was about five at the time, and all I knew then was that it was the most beautiful thing I had ever seen. Dad didn't look so happy as he stepped out and onto the curb. Not really giving that much thought, I asked, "Daddy, did you just buy us a new car? This one is swell. Can we go for a ride? Can we go now?" My questions ran together as I spit them out in my excitement.

Dad looked at me, very sadly, and I wondered if he was going to cry. Looking back at the car, he responded, "No, sweetheart, I didn't just buy this. I just borrowed it for a couple of days, but I have to return it to the dealer this afternoon."

Not understanding, but wishing so much, I asked if I could get in. Dad stepped back to the door, and grabbing the door handle slowly and deliberately, he opened the immense gate to the driver's side and I quickly jumped in.

"Let's go," I cried.

Before Dad could reply, Mom appeared next to the passenger side, and after looking into the car, she looked at me and said, "Enjoy it for a few minutes, Sara, because your Daddy is going to take it back."

As she spoke the last part, she lifted her head back out and looked grimly and knowingly right at my dad. In my mind's eye, I still see Mom's expression; it wasn't one of happiness at all. She wore one of her anger faces and when this face appeared the lines on her forehead were so prominent that even her eyes couldn't help but take on a defensive attitude. Her lips, usually well formed and soft, had all but disappeared into a battle line drawn for the occasion. She was flushed and agitated. Dad was standing up on the sidewalk, looking sheepish and trapped. He tried to talk, but nothing would offer up, and she was ready to talk, or likely yell, but all her vocals were silenced by the vision of that huge car parked in front of them. It may not have mattered that all ten of the parking spaces in front of the store had cars in occupation. Those cars, while in real life were the same size as the convertible, appeared puny and unimportant next to the colossal, exalted roadster that was the subject of the silent flap. The car that might have been ours, that we could have driven in town, in the country, to the grocery, to the pool, to our driveway at home, was not going to happen.

I pictured Mom and Dad in the front seat, dressed in their casual driving clothes, his grey felt fedora and her pheasant pattern silk scarf, and me in the back seat with it all to myself and my toy dog, Robin. None of that happened and at the time I am sure my only reaction was to cry, and slowly, agonizingly slowly, move one inch at a time out of the car.

****

I can now well concoct in my mind the events that led up to the end of the car, creating the conversations and the events that would unravel for Hobby. My imagination has taken me back to that day with it unfolding into the build-up of events, going from the early morning bucolic setting to the end of a summer day that developed turbulence not related to the weather.

What started was a typical Tuesday morning in the store, except that Jessie had earlier rushed around the house getting chores squared away so she could take over the store for Hobby while he went away for the afternoon on a buying trip. Business was brisk and it seemed to her that clothing and shoe inventories were depleted awfully fast and because of this, Hobby either had to go to Luray to get more inventory from his uncle's store or go on to

Fredericksburg to meet with his large suppliers. She couldn't help but wonder why he couldn't consolidate his trips so that he wouldn't have to do this several times a month. It seemed to her that he could easily manage to keep track of inventory and orders. Maybe when he got back today she would talk to him about this, and she could offer to help him keep count of stock. She had a good idea of what was bought and sold since she did most of the check writing for the supplier's merchandise bills; and she helped out in the evening when the store closed to count the day's receipts. She was skilled at this since she had gotten her start as a clerk when his parents owned the store and gained even more experience at the base PX when she and Hobby were in Melbourne, FL during his Navy tour.

Hobby had already left for the afternoon when Jessie arrived just after lunch. Ernie, the long time clerk, was restocking some shelves with shoes. He greeted her and volunteered that they had not really been busy that morning and since the weather was a picture perfect early summer day, likely the store traffic would be slow. Jessie agreed and said that she was going to pay some bills and run them up to the Post Office so they could go out that day. She would be back in the office, if he needed her. Ernie resumed his shoe stocking, but when moments later he heard Jessie open and then slam close the office door, he realized that she hadn't been in there five whole minutes. As he watched, Jessie came up the aisles between the counters, deliberately walking fast with eyes fixed ahead to the door. *Oh boy*, Ernie thought, *that's not good*. Ernie was familiar with Jessie's expressions, and he had witnessed from time-to-time some of the arguments between her and Hobby. He saw an expression not only of determination, but also a hint of a future episode of "What Has Hobby Done Now as Seen by Jessie". And this episode likely would top them all.

Fixing her eyes to zero right in, Jessie confronted the postal clerk and Hobby's cousin, Ralph, at the Post Office.

"Say, Ralph, I didn't know that you had purchased another car. When did this did take place?" she asked.

Ralph, caught off guard, looked away and back, then responded, "Uh, oh, yea, I did get a car a couple of months ago. Haven't even had a chance to tell Mary about it yet."

Jessie squared her stance precisely into his line of vision, and trapped Ralph so he had no choice but to look directly back at her, and said to him, "Ralph, I think you know something that you're not telling me. And, I will find out sooner or later, so you might as well start right now by telling me the truth."

Ralph looked at his feet, and then continued to speak to them as if they could transport his response back up to Jessie. "Gee, Jessie, I wish I could stay and chat with you, but I have to get back to work. The afternoon's mail needs to be put up if it is going out today, and I'm on the clock."

Ralph probably hoped that this response would satisfy Jessie, but she didn't bite and pressed, "Ralph, you are stalling me and I cannot quite understand what the delaying tactic is all about."

She worked hard to keep control of her temper, but it was about to wear as thin as Ralph's excuses for not coming clean.

"The truth, Ralph. What's with the car?" demanded Jessie.

****

Earlier that day, she had gone into the store office looking for the checkbook to pay some bills. As she picked up the checkbook, she bumped against a stack of papers and noticed on top was what appeared to be an insurance policy. She wondered what this was about as she usually handled all of the household and store paperwork, such as taxes, insurance forms, bills, and the like. When she examined the document closer, it turned out to be a policy for a car registered to her in-law, Ralph. It had been marked paid, and a store check number was noted on the bottom. She wondered, *Why would we be paying insurance on a car for Ralph? Why didn't Hobby say something to me?* Since he was away for the afternoon, she decided she would ask Ralph directly about this.

"So, Ralph, let's hear it," Jessie demanded. "Why are we paying the insurance on a car registered in your name?"

Ralph coughed, stammered, and then choked up his version of the truth, "You see, Jessie, it's kind of complicated. I don't really have the car; I mean it's not parked at my house." Ralph knew that he had kept this secret bottled up too long. Jessie's persistence was going to uncover the unsteady lid on this precarious pressure cooker.

Jessie looked through her pocketbook, gave up, and said, "Ralph, let's don't treat me like I'm a fool, okay? I found an insurance policy in Hobby's office, and I know we didn't buy a car. I just want to know why we would pay the insurance for a car that you supposedly own. If Hobby were in town today, believe me I would be confronting him with this, not wasting my time trying to get an honest answer out of you!"
Ralph sat down on one of the benches in the lobby, and motioned to Jessie that she might want to have a seat as well. Spine stiff, she sat, then turned to look at him and said, "Well, I'm all ears."

By this time, Ralph had started to sweat inside his Post Office issued cardigan sweater,. He began. "Jessie, the car is Hobby's. It's not mine. It is kept parked over by the Elkton Restaurant when Hobby is not driving it." There, he had said it. He clasped his hands as much to keep his

81

nerves from collapse, as to keep them from reaching for her hands in some kind of misplaced hope for comfort.

Jessie started to talk, but Ralph held up a hand to Jessie, and said, "Please let me continue. This is important and I wish with all my heart that it wasn't me who was telling you this. Hobby is not on a buying trip, he is up in Shenandoah visiting with Marge." Ralph, now liberated, gathered strength and continued, "He uses the car to drive there so that no one will recognize him. Hobby knows that everyone recognizes his blue Dodge pickup truck so with this car he could slip over to Verbena Tavern and visit Marge."

With that, Ralph exhaled, looked at Jessie, and then out of air looked down at the floor.

Jessie was stunned, but reached over to Ralph and patted his arm. She softly said, "Ralph, it's alright. I don't blame you. I can see that you were doing this to help Hobby. He put you in a pretty crappy position. I appreciate you being honest with me. Now, do you happen to know when Hobby is due back?"

Ralph realized that he was not quite off-the-hook, and offered, "He's due back about six-thirty this evening."
Ralph reached for her hand on his arm, said, "Jessie I am so sorry to be the one to tell you all this. Please forgive me."

Jessie shook his hand off gently, stood up, and walked out the door into the afternoon. As she headed back to the store, she composed her thoughts as to how she would confront Hobby with her new found knowledge. She had a hundred questions going through her head, but she wanted to keep her head straight for what surely would be a major fight.

Late in the afternoon, Hobby returned back to the parking lot next to the restaurant, found his usual space available and with the sun playing tag with big heavy clouds he was pleased that no one saw him or associated him with the yellow convertible he just slid out of. He had a most wonderful afternoon, and was still feeling good as he walked down the street to the store. When he came through the door, there were just a couple of customers finishing up their purchases. He saw Jessie walk from the office up to the front; and when she got up to the counter where he had set his briefcase, she had a big smile and with all the love she could muster, she asked, "How was the buying trip?"

Just then the phone rang, and Ernie answered it, looked over to Hobby, and said, "It's for you, it's Ralph."

"Tell Ralph I'll call him back in a couple of minutes," Hobby replied, and still smiling, clueless Hobby turned back, and responded to Jessie, "Great, it was just great."

Some days later this storm, too, had passed and another of their many truces had been accepted. Civility returned, flares were extinguished, and Dad's business trips ended. The peace treaty did not go without some visible evidence of its existence. The new car that my mom drove, while not as magnificent as the yellow convertible, was grand in its own way—cream colored, with a brown hard top—Desoto coupe with lots of chrome, white wall tires, and a very large back seat perfect for me, Ernie, and my toys. Mom drove the new car everywhere and when she worked at the store, she parked it right in front.

The Zen of Cootie

I learned a valuable life lesson as a little girl, and at the time, I didn't even realize the lesson. It never occurred to me that I learned the lesson from a game about a molded plastic insect called "Cootie." Without this little game, I would not have appreciated the chance to bond with my father, nor would I have learned how much fun it was to share playing a game with him. My problem was that he won at playing Cootie, and all I could do was seethe in my little girl way at losing.

****

Games have been historically great ways to teach interaction with children and to assist them in learning socialization skills. To learn how to win and to lose, accepting both with grace, dignity, and humility is a tall order for someone who is about six years old. But then again one cannot start too soon to teach youngsters appropriate social behavior that will stay with them all their lives. Such may have been the intent with my parents as they acquired games for me to play. These games came on the heels of my having listened, since the cradle, to the phonograph playing the hit recording, "Please and Thank-You."

I had no siblings to play with, so the regular gamers were my parents. While I certainly never saw my folks play games, much less Cootie, with each other, I sought them out to play with me. It seemed when I played with my mother, I often won. When I played with my father, I never did. Dad didn't play any other parlor-type games that I recall. Possibly he played Monopoly with me a time or two, I am not sure. And, there were no photographs that recorded any games played between father and daughter, or even mother and daughter.

So, what about Cootie made it attractive to play? First of all, it came in a brightly colored box, with sections inside that held the body parts waiting for assembly. One section held eight antennae, one held all twenty-four of the legs (six per body), four bodies, four heads, four hats (boys), four bows (girls), eight eyes, four swirly tongues and lips. The assembly of a Cootie was based on the roll of a die. For instance, a player started with the body; and a player needed to role a "1" before any other parts were added. Once the "1" was rolled, the player continued with his turn to roll for other parts. After that key starting roll, every following roll was bound to get the player something useful. A head was the "2"; the antennae, bows and hats were the "3"; the eyes were the "4"; the lips and tongue were the"5"; and legs were the "6." If a player kept the roll, based on rolling a number that matched a needed body part, then that player's chance of winning greatly improved. The whole idea was to complete the assembly of a Cootie before the opponent. The game was so simple that printed directions were not even in the box. Everything that was needed was on the outside of the box itself. Somehow, though, I believed that there was a deeper level of complexity about Cootie.

It was always with great enthusiasm and no shortage of confidence that I invited my father to play a round of Cootie when he came home from the store. And it was always with confidence that I would announce that the roller of the highest number would go first. With this same confidence I generally lost the first roll, but still encouraged, I remained optimistic that I would complete my Cootie first. Dad had tremendous luck at rolling the die. He typically managed to keep on rolling and building up his little plastic insect well ahead of my attempts. I was convinced that he held strategy secrets or that he secretly practiced when I was not around.

Even when I got aggressive with the die during one particular game, I did not improve my luck to close the assembly gap. Dad managed to stay happy in this game, and I recall that he encouraged me; but by that time, I was steaming inside, and secretly building up my own personal storm.

I was too young and inexperienced to grasp any finesse at Cootie strategy, so I relied simply on my own skill set at the time. This set consisted of mostly choosing the color body I wanted to assemble, believing that certain colors, red and blue, had some basic instinctive capability of getting finished first. Dad, because he was much older, likely had learned much more about the finer plays and maneuvers of winning at Cootie. Maybe he even had a secret book with tips on how to assemble a winning Cootie faster than an opponent. All I knew was that whatever I did, I was not going to match his ability to roll just the right part number every time and finish his Cootie first. I did not then learn the lesson of losing gracefully, as I erupted that bottled up steam into a full blown temper tantrum and stalked off.

Dad was probably flabbergasted. Mom, having heard all of this take place in the dining room from her vantage point in the kitchen, came through the doorway, looked at Dad, then headed off to find me. For his part, Dad asked Mom what he had done wrong? All he was doing was rolling a die and trying to assemble his Cootie. Watching her back, he saw Mom nod her head up and down in understanding. When she found me, I was up in my room, on my bed, crying to my cat. In my hand, I was holding a Cootie antenna..

She sat down on the edge of the bed, and as she dried her hands on her apron, she spoke softly to me, saying that my father wouldn't want to play Cootie with me if I was going to be such a sore loser. Didn't I want to play games with my dad? What kind of daughter would he think he had if he couldn't relax and play with me? Was I concerned that I possibly hurt his feelings?

I recall looking up at her, eyes streaming, nose running, realizing that nothing could be worse than him not wanting to play with me anymore. I managed to choke up a sorry and she suggested that I come back down and tell him. When we got back downstairs, Dad was carefully packing away the Cootie game. He looked at me and didn't say anything, but slowly started taking the parts back out of the box. I sat down across from him, and without so much as a sigh or sound, I picked up the die. Before I rolled, I handed it over to him, and said he could go first. I offered that he could have first choice on body color, too. He took the die, looked into the kitchen at Mom, then back at me.

Cooties are supposed to represent the insect family since they have six legs and antennae. The lips and tongues and hats are just for our amusement in the game. Most members of the insect family are social, relying on group cooperation to survive. In many insect societies, there are different individuals assigned to do different tasks. These are genetically programmed and never change. Humans are not bound by such rigid genetic make-up. Humans make choices and can change actions to suit the circumstances. Humans have emotions; and as far as science knows, insects do not.

When a Cootie is fully assembled, it looks just like something one would see in a comic book or cartoon. The eyes have a goofy, happy shape; and when it is completed the whole Cootie looks happy.

Ernie Can't Play Poker

The game of Poker mirrors some parts of life. For example, I have heard many times in many settings, having nothing to do with Poker, the phrase, "a card laid, is a card played." This has been always presented in the context of once one has committed an action, one has to live with the consequences. I assumed the phrase came from a card game like Poker. In Poker there are laws, such as general laws which apply to the shuffle, the deal, the cut, the pack of cards and the rank of cards themselves. There are laws that deal with irregularities, such as misdeals, exposed cards, an incorrect pack, and betting. These laws and descriptions all work to minimize the damage of improprieties during Poker play.

Poker was a good model to describe the part of my mom's life when card playing was a major form of recreation for her. Morehead's book, *Official Rules of Card Games,* discussed Poker's rise in popularity[in the hundred or so years leading up to 1968] when millions discovered that Poker held a great "appeal to ladies" and that this same game could be understood by nearly every American. Part of Poker's charm was its easiness to learn and its enjoyable play. Whether it started during the time when Dad was in the Navy, or when Mom held her regular card games in the house years later, when she had a young child, Poker

91

or any kind of card playing really was one of the pleasures of life for her. It wasn't so much about winning money as it was about simply winning.

When Mom had learned to play Poker is a moot point as her ability to grasp the fine points of playing and betting must have come easily to her. On the other hand, Ernie, the store's long time clerk and family friend, must have never mastered the minor points, much less the finer points, as he seldom, if ever won at Mom's card table. Yet, he kept coming back. He was the first to arrive to play and the last to leave, every time. I don't think it was ever about Poker for Ernie. I think it was about my mother.

****

During their Navy years, one of my mom's favorite activities was playing cards, particularly Poker. She became famous among her husband's fellow photography school attendees for her weekly Poker games. I suspect that she seldom lost, talented with an innate ability to count cards played and anticipate future deals from the deck. The games were always lively and convivial, supported by some drinking, good-natured betting, and ribbing over lost or won hands. My dad did not join in the card games. He preferred to take pictures of his friends and wife, active and intent on gaining their own upper hands. The friendship bonds made during those playful times meant a great deal to her and Dad; and some of these same friends stayed in contact for many years long beyond the Navy time.

As I remember my youthful experience with my mother's card playing in Elkton, I recall that the regular meetings started on Saturday nights about 10p.m., and lasted until about 7a.m. the following morning. The participants varied through the years, with some being brothers-in-law, brothers, sisters-in-law, store patrons, local friends, and the always present Ernie. I think that this weekly card game was the only social event of Ernie's life. He lived with his sister, having lost his twin brother just after high school in a car accident. He had started out working for my dad's father in the same store that Dad later inherited. He had never known any other employment, except for one brief stint at the Farm Bureau. He was more of a fixture in the store than the cash register; and he was just as much a fixture at the card games.

****

Ernie's loyalty to the family stretched all the way back to his youth. Both he and his brother, Everett, had worked for my grandfather in the store when they were teenagers. Mostly sweeping in the store, gathering trash, and washing the store windows, they grew up in the store just as much as my dad and sisters had. Ernie's family lived in town up on Rockingham Street, and he walked to work from there.

Ernie and his brother were active in local sports, especially baseball. While Ernie many not have grasped all the rules and nuances of Poker, it was generally accepted that no one knew more about baseball than Ernie. My grandfather likely supplied some of the clothing or at least some monies to help finance uniforms or equipment. Even Ernie's nephew, William (aka Billy and Red) spent time in the store. I remember his afternoon visits when he came in from high school to see his uncle and talk baseball and other sports.

Red lived with Ernie and his sister for a while, too. The devastation to the family from Everett's death lasted many years, but Red seemed to fill the void a little. Ernie never talked about his brother and the only way I knew anything about him was from my parents.

After Dad's father died and Dad took over the store, there had not been any question that Ernie would remain as clerk. Dad needed Ernie and he would not have left the store for anything. It was his home, too, and his anchor. I often thought, as I became older and more aware, that the reason Ernie stayed was because he was in love with my mother. It was hard to tell who he might have been more loyal to, her or my dad. For many years, Ernie covered for my dad in his extra-curricular activities, and this must have been terrible for him if he was indeed in love with my mom.

Each Poker player is responsible for his own hand and has no redress if another player causes a card in it to be exposed. [Morehead]

****

Sometime before I started first grade and until at least the start of high school, my mom had her regular Saturday night Poker games. These happened once or twice a

95

month, and they were always colorful, if not somewhat turbulent, events. She had a ritual preparation before the games and the central focus of that ritual was the arrangement of the table in the dining room and positioning of the chairs. She had a special tablecloth (allowing for ease of sliding cards) and other accessories-ashtrays, coasters, and the like.

She bought ahead of time at least two new packs of cards, one red and one blue, which she would leave unopened until everyone arrived, got their beverages, and their seats, and counted either their chips or their coins. I can imagine her during the preparation holding the decks lovingly, touching the cellophane wrapper with reverence, setting them on the table, picking them up, setting them down again. She might be thinking about who would be coming to play, where he/she would sit, what the general mood would be. I don't think she wondered about what Dad or I was doing. He would have gone to bed to read and sleep; I would have gone to my room with my cat to read, listen to the radio, and then sleep.

Sometimes I made more money, as I slept, than some of the players. We had two recliner chairs in the living room and some of the men would sit in them on a break from playing. Their loose change would fall out from their trouser pockets into the folds of the chairs. This was a treasure hunt for me the next day, and I always felt like I had won the pot. Mom did not make me give the money back since she would not know from whose pants the money had parted.

The players would arrive and Mom would greet them, generally about five fellows. Sometimes Aunt Lillian (Dad's sister) would join them. They'd get their drinks, smokes, some snacks, then find their seats. Each player brought out his/her special Poker cash pouch and commenced the ritual sorting of the coins. Money would be stacked by coin type, followed by discussion of the betting amounts, ending with the ante to the pot.

Before the cards are even dealt, the rules of the Poker game being played require that each player put an initial contribution(called an ante)of one or more chips(coins)into the pot, to start off. [Morehead]

There wasn't a starting bell to signal the first deal or play, but all eyes turned to my mom in anticipation of the start. She reached down and picked up the first deck, maybe the blue one. She started slowly pulling the red cellophane strip that opened the entire wrapper, liberating the card deck. I'm certain she smiled slightly at the pack as she removed the cards from the box. And then she handed the deck off to Ernie to be shuffled. She next picked up a second pack, and repeated the ritual. Still all the eyes were on her. She would shuffle this second deck, feeling the stiff, pristine cards; somehow she sensed the impending liberation of the individual cards that would ultimately form loosely organized regimens of chance. Attempts to mate cards or numerically line some up in sequence awaited all the participants, poised hopefully for the first deal of the night. At last she would pick one of the decks, perhaps the red, and ask one of the players to "cut. "As she looked at each player in turn, she would deal each the requisite card.

Mom seldom lost at poker; and when she lost, it wasn't much. She had a limited, but notorious reputation, for her ability to win. She had great stamina and staying power for the duration; and it was not unusual for others just to give out, give up, and go home.

Whenever only one active player remains, through every other players' having dropped, the active player wins the pot without showing [her] hand, and there is a new deal by the next dealer in turn. [Morehead]

Sometimes the losers weren't always in good humor, and I remembered being woken up on several occasions by one participant who shouted out that he was losing too much and that it wasn't fair. He demanded that he be allowed to change seats to see if his luck would change.

After the start of the game no player may demand a reseating unless at least one hour has elapsed since the last reseating. [Morehead]

Since most of the regulars had their usual spots at the table, this player was not successful with this tactic. He was known to drink a bit much at these games and when he did his losses took on enormous proportions in his mind. This was unlikely since they were playing mostly "penny ante" and quarter max bets. But in all fairness, the pots added up to dollars and the dollars would add up as well, so a possible evening/morning loss could reach to twenty-five to thirty dollars. In the 1950's this was not insignificant, especially spent on a game of chance.

Ernie always lost. No matter the version of poker being played or where he sat around the table. I can't remember a single time where I ever heard that he had won. He likely had the worst card sense of anyone playing, but he never dropped out.

Conservatism pays in Poker, and in a game with expert players it is necessary. The general rule is: You should stay in only in either of two cases: (a) you believe you have the best hand, or (b) the odds against your drawing the best hand are less than the odds offered by the pot. [Morehead]

Ernie gave it all he had and he lost all he had, which was his weekly paycheck. It was ironic that the following Monday Dad gave Ernie his weekly pay back along with a carton of Winston cigarettes. Then the cycle would start all over again when the next Saturday night came around.

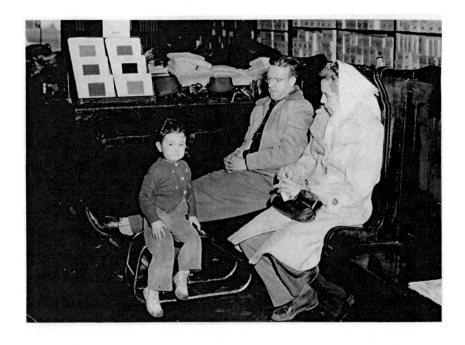

Mom shut down her poker games after one particular incident that involved me. On what would be the last night, I woke suddenly to shouting, clashing of chairs, more cursing, slamming of doors, and even the sound of what might have been glass fracturing. I ran down the stairs, battle ready in flannel pajamas with teeth clenched, found a broom, and amidst the din, yelled my best. I chased everyone out of the dining room and the house, as I waved my weapon. While I aimed mostly at the men, even Mom was forced to retreat to safety. It's amazing how a ten year old can scatter adults.

After the scene quieted, and the players left, Mom took my hand and led me back to my room. For his part, Ernie stayed to help clean up. Even more amazing was that Dad never appeared, and he likely slept through the entire episode. The next day Mom and Dad had a big conversation that did not include me, and when the next Saturday arrived, Mom announced that she was going to a friend's to play bridge.

After Mom shut down her poker night, Ernie tried poker at my Uncle Kenny's(Aunt Lillian's husband) pool hall, but he lost there, too. Only in that location those losses were gone forever. The only exception was when my boyfriend at that time played. He was a regular at those poker games and was known to win a lot of the time. When Dad heard later that the boyfriend had played and that Ernie had lost, Dad gave Ernie back his losses and of course, a carton of cigarettes. My folks didn't care for my boyfriend much.

Even in the last years of his employment when his eyesight faltered, and he wasn't able to add or subtract so well; and, even hearing the times that Dad complained to Mom and me that Ernie was costing him money in lost sales and miscalculations, Dad kept him on. Some of my teenage arguments with Dad were about why he was keeping Ernie at the store. Dad argued back that I didn't understand, and he was right. Dad kept him because of Mom and loyalty.

In some games, a player may do anything to fool his opponents so long as he does not cheat. [Morehead]

Ernie continued to clerk at the store until he retired, long after I had left home and on my own. For over forty-one years he worked for my father and during all this time, I don't think he ever said a bad word about him or my mom. While there weren't many pictures of Ernie among all the ones that my dad took, there were two pictures that I recall the best. One was in the store with him sitting on a bench seat with my mom and me sitting in front of them on a stool. Both of them were looking at me as I looked at Dad, who took the picture. The second one was of him from one of Dad's books, and he modeled a sport coat for an ad for the store that Dad composed. He looked remarkably like Woody Allen. If he played, Woody probably never lost at poker.

I don't remember the year that Ernie died. I recall he died of a heart attack; and it might have even occurred in his sleep. I didn't see him much when I returned home for visits. He didn't come down to the store anymore, and he seemed to have dropped out of Mom and Dad's lives as they all aged. If they ever talked about Ernie, I wasn't around to hear about it. Mom still played cards, mostly bridge and spite-and-malice, including the week she died.

Since card playing is a social pastime, a player is best advised to follow the standards of the other players and remain popular. [Morehead]

The Black Hawk Waltz

One desire in my life has been to hear my mother play "The Black Hawk Waltz" just one more time. I was imprinted with the memory of that music as much as a nestling bird, just out of its shell, was imprinted with its own mother's unique song. When I was a little kid, she played this waltz so often on the piano we had in the living room, I thought the piano played it by itself. I'm sure she played other music, but I only remember that one. I don't recall anyone who visited and asked her to play it. I just remember asking her to play that song that I liked and she would know which one I meant. Sometimes I sat on the bench with her as she moved her fingers easily on the faded ivory keyboard.

She had the softest hands, with impeccable short nails that were seldom polished. And it was not that the fingers were especially long, pianist fingers. They were shapely, but not too soft. She did her own housework with her own hands. It was just that when she played, the fingers seemed not to have any trouble reaching all the notes. She manicured her nails so she knew all the particular parts and capabilities of her fingers. Her tools were emery boards, cuticle snippers, special shaped sticks and tiny little scissors. These were prized possessions and I marveled at the time she spent grooming her fingers. She didn't wear much jewelry on her hands, just her wedding band and a watch and occasionally a necklace. As much as I watched her fingers, I don't know when she stopped wearing her wedding band. Sometime in my youth she took her band off and didn't wear it anymore. I know she didn't lose it, as I have it today among my jewelry pieces.

When she performed the Black Hawk Waltz, the left and right hands played different notes; and with her right hand as she went through the progression she would arch her wrist, raise back her fingers, then they would go back to the keyboard to repeat the sequence. She could easily coordinate the left hand part with the right hand part without looking at the keys, with any intensity masked by a slight smile. She would repeat the whole progression with its unusual finger movements many times.

I don't know when or why she stopped playing the waltz, any music, or the piano. I just remember that the piano became the base for holding books, pictures, and the occasional Christmas tree. All the prior music was silenced and trapped within the cover over the sleeping keys. Then one day the piano itself was gone, and for several empty years, until my parents got an upright for my piano lessons, there was no waltz sound or any other piano sound to be heard. For the years of my life gone by, I have relied on my memory of bits and pieces of the tune to conjure up the memory of her playing The Black Hawk Waltz.

****

The Black Hawk Waltz is an old parlor piece written by Mary Walsh back in the late 1800's. From what I learned it was often played at family gatherings; and many in my generation have remembered it as played by grandmothers as well as mothers. The piece itself is an interesting mix of tempos, starting from a light and breezy rising waltz; and then in the second and subsequent movements it quickly gathers speed only to stop and revert to the waltz part again. This music is sweet and cunning at the same time. To me it was a mesmerizing complex musical score. The mystery of that waltz's composition was not unlike the mystery that was my mother.

Very little is known about the composer, Mary E. Walsh. What is known is that she was educated by the Sisters of Notre Dame, NY. Recently, many years after her death, she was acknowledged to be the author of a most popular hymn that is found in most Catholic hymnals, called "Bring Flowers of the Fairest." Likely she composed more music and wrote more words than can be attributed to her. The most popular of her works has been The Black Hawk Waltz. Original covers of the sheet music actually had artwork of Chief Black Hawk, the American Indian who survived the Black Hawk War of 1832. After being released from imprisonment he took what remained of his tribe and family and settled in Iowa, where he died in 1838. Apparently after the war Chief Black Hawk became somewhat of a folk hero, and notes found state that Mary Walsh wrote this piece in honor of him. There were no lyrics, only the musical score. With all this then, Mary Walsh herself remains a mystery.

How did such a charming piece of music find its way into parlors and music halls around the turn of the century?

How did someone like my mother find this music and learn how to play it? And, play it memorably? The song was published in 1897, thirteen years before my mother was even born. Maybe it was one of the first songs she learned. Perhaps she had a music teacher and since this was one of the popular choices for music teachers to use, this was how she learned it. Maybe she played it for her parents and friends in their homes. As far as I knew, her sister Myrtle was the only other sibling who played this waltz, too. I remember asking her to play it for me on her piano when I was in college. While I loved to hear her play it as well, the effect was not the same. These two sisters played the same song, but with such difference that this was as good a key as any to tell them apart. Myrtle could only play Myrtle's rendition and my mom could only play hers.

How many of us recall a musical tune or bit from back in our childhood? If we could, did we know how we associated the music? Was it connected to some event that brought us happiness? Or was it associated with something that made us sad? Whenever I would hear my Mother start to play that song, no matter what I was doing or where I was that I could hear it, I would come back to the house as fast as I could to not miss any of that waltz. My child brain with its memory sponge unfolding and expanding, captured everything that was in its path, like the little trick sponges I got at the dime store that became a pink fish or a green dinosaur. I memorized that tune and all its parts as faithfully as I memorized the multiplication tables. While I wasn't musically inclined like my mom, the one musical attribute I learned was to listen intently. And that gave me the lasting memory of that lilting waltz.

When she stopped playing it, apparently for good, I didn't ask her why. I guess I was too young to ask and I just accepted the discontinuance as fact. I didn't cry, and perhaps I didn't mourn. When she signed me up for piano lessons, which I really didn't want to take, she never suggested I learn to play that song.

She didn't sit by me as I struggled to learn piano notes and transport notes from paper to piano key. She had the natural talent to play and read music. She could sit still whereas I could not.

But if I remember The Black Hawk Waltz so well, after all these years, then she must have played it a lot when I was very young. And, now, it is too late for me to talk to her about the Black Hawk. I'll never know why she stopped playing it, and now I search the internet for all the ways I can hear it. I've downloaded a couple of versions, and even the discords in the middle of the piece don't seem out of place or even awkward. Composer Walsh must have put them in there for a reason. Could it have been that she didn't want the music to be perfect? I can't learn to play the piece myself, but I do listen carefully to it. I don't listen for the possible flaws. I listen simply to hear it. When I do,

I fall easily into recalling the Mother of my youth, intent on the keys, left hand playing the keys maintaining the waltz beat, the right hand finessing the higher notes. The sound of the piano filled the living room of our house and found a way to escape out the front door into the yard.

I have recalled her at that time at peace for the moments of that song, separate from the drama of her marriage and separate from the challenge of raising a child. She and I were at peace for the moments as well. No battles with a child on the horizon. No surrenders. We both had just the space and time of this almost forgotten little gift of music from a little known composer who did not know how much of an impact her powerful waltz had on those who played it, those who loved to listen to it, and one who longed to hear her Mother engage the music once more.

Hattie Mae

Splashing around in the tub, I eagerly waited for her to come and bathe me. This was the first bath for me in a couple of days as I had been sick with the chicken pox. For days Mom soaked me in that awful floating oatmeal stuff; and I longed to have my skin back to normal. I wanted Hattie Mae and the magical bar of Ivory soap. Mom wouldn't let Hattie Mae come to the house while I was contagious, but now I was safe, she said. The doctor had told her yesterday that Hattie could come back, and in separate rooms in the house, our sighs of relief were in perfect synchrony, even if we didn't know it.

I loved for Hattie Mae to give me my bath. I watched as she drew the water into the tub. That's how the ritual began. Soap and warm water did magical things under the spell of her fingers. She hummed some private tune; and the water, temperature perfect, was coaxed right out of the faucet. She would add some bubble bath kept in the bathroom for sensitive skin. When she deemed the water and soap bubble levels just right, she called to me and I ran from my room and paused by her side. Gently helping me take off my clothes, she lifted me over and in. Next she pulled out towels, washcloth, and a big pristine bar of Ivory soap from the dresser in the bathroom. As she knelt down her considerable, toffee-colored body, she began to soap up the washcloth. It was a wonderful slow process and the contrast of her dark skin to the white of the soap and the pink of my skin was hypnotic to me. The contrasts of the colors were the same as my favorite ice cream, Neapolitan. As the soap built its own bubbly lather it ran in rivulets on the tops of her hands, through her fingers, into the cloth and onto my skin; it was the most tranquil mesmerizing sensation for me; and the most loving ritual of my day. And from that time in my life forward, I loved that color of skin, Ivory soap, and when she was no longer in my life, my memory of Hattie Mae.

****

We tormented the heck out of her. We loved her yet we were mischievous; constantly hiding from her or jumping out from behind a couch or door screeching our best, just to watch how high she would jump. I could not do any of this by myself, so I would enlist my childhood best friends, Linda and Jim to join me in the daily acts of driving Miss Hattie crazy. With the games underway we ran all over the house, through the kitchen, out the back porch, under the back porch, back through the living room door, and finally settled into exhaustion in my room. When we heard her heavy steps on the stairs, accompanied by calling for us, we remained silent and pretended we were reading comic books when she looked into the room. She would scold us; oh, she would scold us about running through the house. Didn't we know better? We hung our heads acting like we were sorry and full of remorse; she knew better. Then she just stood there, ample arms across equally ample bosom, fingers tapping. We couldn't look at her, but then she couldn't see our grins either. After what seemed like days, she turned around with a sigh of, "um, um, um...."

Next we heard her call, "Lunch will be ready in ten minutes, you little hellions. You'd better wash up and get on down to the kitchen if you want a hamburger."
We lived for those...her hamburgers. They were the best, and we didn't have to ask for them. She always knew. Linda and Jim could always stay for lunch on hamburger day, which was Saturday. And, she fixed pork-n-beans, too. This was the life. Summers with Hattie Mae, Linda, and Jim were the best.

When it was just her and me, she read to me and told me stories about her family. I loved the stories about her mother, Etta, and their house out at Newtown. I rode with my mother in the morning to pick up Hattie Mae and then again in the afternoon when Mom took her home. I saw other kids playing in their backyard; and they had farm animals, too.

Because I had ongoing battles between being well and sick, I didn't get to stay and play until I was a little older. One day when we were on the way to pick up Hattie Mae, Mom surprised me by asking if I wanted to spend the day at Etta's. I was thrilled and when we got there, I jumped out of the car so fast I forgot to tell my mother good-bye. Hattie Mae shouted to me to turn and wave good-bye, but by that time, Mom had already disappeared behind the dust that followed her back to the main road. I waved anyway, and then turned and came into the house. Etta had called from the kitchen for me to come on back there. When I entered the kitchen, which was larger than any I had ever seen, I was hit suddenly by the most wonderful profusion of aromas. I picked out ham and some things that were very sweet. Etta patted a chair and pointed to me to come over and sit down.

"I have something real special for you, little girl," she said. In her hand was a basket with a cloth in it covering something, and when she took this cloth off, there remained the most remarkable stack of biscuits. They were plump, golden, and almost too pretty to eat. She set the basket down on the table, picked out a big biscuit from within, cut it in half and with a wooden knife loaded with butter, began to spread on each side a wide swath. To each side she added a slice of ham.

She looked at me, eyes twinkling, and asked, "Would you like some honey for these?"

I wished then I could have died right there on the spot. "Sure, please, Miss Etta," I replied.

In trying to remember that day, I have convinced myself that I ate at least a half a dozen of those biscuits. The basket had seemed never ending and no one told me to stop eating. I think I only stopped when Hattie Mae's nieces and nephews showed up to play with me. We spent the rest of the morning playing cars and tractors on the kitchen floor, out on the front porch, and in the front yard. We ran around the house, confined to the outside here. When we tired of that, we went out to the back buildings and looked at the chickens and cows. There were dogs and cats, too. We chased them around and they chased us. We climbed trees and fences, picked buttercups to prove we all loved butter, and we hid in the pasture from imaginary villains.

Etta had a big bell on her back porch which she used to call everyone in for lunch. Adults and children stopped whatever they were doing and headed back to the house. On this day, Etta had fried up a huge batch of chicken and made potato salad to go with it. There was nothing like the aroma of fried chicken reaching all around, inviting you to touch your lips on salt-and-peppered crispy skin and to sink your teeth into tender, moist thigh meat. It was heaven for me. I hadn't had fried chicken in what seemed like years.

One of the grown men, Garfield, asked if there were any biscuits left from breakfast and Etta, his mother, said she had set some aside for him. She also surprised us all by bringing over to the table a large bowl of gravy. I watched Garfield take two biscuits, open them slowly, and place them in the middle of his plate. Next he took a large soup spoon and dipped it into the gravy; and as if he were leading an orchestra, he directed with great precision and timing the deposit of multiple spoons-full of the giblet-laden sauce right on them. Breaking from the trance, I did exactly the same thing. That was the day I learned what it meant to savor a good meal. Etta smiled at everyone and when she finally came to the table, she sat by me. As she chose her favorite piece of chicken, she looked at me and said, "I think you've had a pretty good day so far, don't you."

Mouth still full, cheeks bulging, I did manage to reply, "Yes, m'am. Thank you, Miss Etta."

That afternoon we all napped in various spots around the house. After she washed me up a little better, Hattie Mae and I napped in her room on the shady side of the house. She had a big double bed with a cast iron headboard shaped like fence railing. It was cool to the touch and I rested my head against it for a bit. We looked at magazines until we dozed off, my head on her lap and her arms across my shoulders. One of the cats had come up, settled in at the foot of the bed and purred itself to sleep. I dreamt of chickens flying around the house with us kids trying to catch them with little lassos. Garfield and Etta were laughing and urging us on. Hattie Mae was waving a frying pan telling us to hurry. We couldn't catch them for anything.

Mom came for me later and all the way home I told her everything we had done; and what all I had eaten. I told her about chicken gravy and how I had learned to put it on biscuits. She asked me how many biscuits I had eaten, and I lied, saying I had eaten only one. I don't know why I lied. I guess I just wanted something of that day to stay a secret. I asked her what she had done all day while I was in the country. She told me that she and Dad had taken a little trip to Luray. She wished she had gotten chicken.

Repairing Irons

The aroma of something sweet, perhaps, too, a little pungent or sharp, would sneak out from the slightly opened and tilted window, slip across their backyard, and drift around the old walnut tree. This same wisp rose on an orphaned summer thermal left from the day into the raised and waiting window of my bedroom, ignored my closed eyes, touched my anxious forehead, entered my nose as I drifted off, and left me smiling with my last awakened thought...*Ah, Mr. Rouse is working tonight.*

From underneath their house in a basement that had been built and finished to accommodate a work bench, tools, stools, shelves, boxes of nuts, bolts, screws, cords, plugs, wires, spare parts, Mr. Rouse would begin his nightly ritual of repairing some household appliance. Such ritual was one of the most fulfilling palliatives of my youth. Half facing the Rouse's house, which had originally belonged to my grandparents, my room was my own secret portal to their lives. Especially, it was a portal to the basement. When Mr. Rouse was working, the outside storm door that led down to the basement would be open, which meant that if one needed something repaired, one just showed up with the object and went down the cement stairs and into the workshop. Mr. Rouse repaired all types of electrical appliances, clocks, irons, toasters, waffle irons, vacuum

cleaners, and the like. For some special customers, he would repair bicycles, tricycles, pogo sticks, doll baby carriages, toy cars, lawnmowers and whatever else that would be considered for minor repairs.

I loved going down in that basement and watching him work. He would bring over a stool for me to sit on close to his work area and then he would set about repairing something. Maybe it was an iron at the time that needed a new cord. Or maybe its heating element didn't work. He would slowly, methodically take it apart, laying all the parts neatly together. He would sometimes look up and point out something to me. Then he would go back to his task. I was transfixed by the whole process. A radio always played low in the background. I can't remember what kind of music, but probably it was popular standards of the 1950's. I can't see him listening to what I did which was Wolfman Jack out of New York City, playing all the rock and roll hits of the 50's. But the music he had on fit what he was doing, and while I sat there I liked the music very much.

He didn't hum along or anything, and to him maybe the radio didn't even exist, but if repairing irons and clocks were set to music, then what he chose is what I would have picked. I could just barely hear that radio when I would be up in my room, and that along with the basement light, the perfume of his work elixir (his special whiskey), and the soft clink of tools he set down and picked up would lull me right into the elusive and precious sleep.

****

Sleep had not always come easily for me as a child. Troubled for many years by a cantankerous stomach, I was nauseous just about every night when put to bed. To that point, my mom generally had to put newspapers or a bucket along side of my bed in preparation for what was known to come. I was afraid to fall asleep, burdened with the unsettled feeling that I was doomed to be interrupted by yet another night of nauseous misery. Cries out in the night would bring my mom into the room where once again she would discover the products of my distress. Soothing washcloths, wet and cold, would be hurriedly brought in, applied, removed, re-applied, to the teeth-chattering, whimpering mess that was me. What could comfort a child that was sick most of the time? What finally has to happen to give relief to child and parents? How long does an ordeal like this continue? I am sure that my parents must have asked these questions and more, trying to understand and give relief and comfort.

Multiple trips to the doctor, multiple shots, multiple things to drink, everything from laxatives to antacids to ginger ale were administered all in the hope that something would drive those gastric demons away. Nothing really worked. Ultimately I learned to hate orange juice, because it only seemed to come with castor oil in it. I became scared of shots and even the doctor. What helped a kid feel better in that case? When I felt good, I played a lot around the house and yard. When I was sick, I just stayed in my room, coloring or reading.

When I was old enough that Mom and Dad could spend their days at the store, they hired a colored lady, Hattie Mae, to take care of me and the house. But mostly she was there to take care of me. Sometimes she stayed the night during the week. I liked that, but I still got sick. I can remember her giving me baths and how I liked the white foam of Ivory soap lathered up on her dark skin. She would hum low in her throat some old songs that I had heard at our own church as she bathed me; and I can remember not feeling so sick when I was in the bath. She read to me and we colored together and I always went with my mom when we took Hattie Mae home at the end of the day. I sometimes went to her house where she lived with her mom, Etta. The cooking smells were tantalizing and agreeable to me. When I would spend the day out there I could eat whatever Etta fixed. Etta had one of those old-fashioned heavy wood-burning cook stoves. And, something was always either cooking on top or just about to come out of the oven below. Her biscuits were announced by an aroma that reached halfway to town, if permitted to last that long. Eager mouths from Hattie's brothers and sisters cut short any chance that someone outside the house would find the treasure in there.

When Hattie Mae left us to get married, her sister Peggy came to take over the household chores and the watching of me. By this time, I was late childhood, around eleven or twelve. I was in grade school during the week, so Saturday was the only day Peggy was needed. I didn't get sick so much, but I still had my bouts. Sleep still eluded me, but I was improving. Peggy taught me how to "Shag" dance and how to practice with the fridge handle when I was by myself, my Frigidaire dance partner. She loved music and showed me where all the great rock-n-roll stations were on the AM dial. At night, I could listen to WOWO, "Wonderful WoWo"; WBZ in Chicago; WABC and Wolfman Jack in NYC; Charlotte, NC; and others. I learned all about Elvis, the Shirrelles, the Temptations, the Ponytails, the Lettermen, and so on.

Gradually Peggy's time with us slipped away, fewer Saturdays, and then she left for Washington for her career. Her cousin Kathleen came for a short time, but as I was closing in on thirteen, my parents decided I was now able to stay at home alone on Saturdays. By now I cleaned house and helped out at the store. The battles with my stomach had subsided a great deal.

122

****

But while I was young, things had changed at my neighbor's house as well. Mr. Rouse worked less at Merck so he had started this little appliance repair business in his basement. Sometimes Mrs. Rouse had pinched in and helped take care of me so I spent much time at their house. I remembered her giving me hot dogs on buns with mustard out of a plastic bottle dispenser that I squeezed in the middle. At my house, the mustard was always in a glass jar. I directed the plastic bottle as if it were a magic marker to spell out names. Sometimes I spelled Mom; sometimes I spelled my cat's name; sometimes I spelled Nellie (Mrs. Rouse); but most of the time, I spelled Jack (Mr. Rouse). They let me ride my bikes and scooters in their driveway and on their sidewalks. I mastered my pogo stick down and back their front yard sidewalk. I was given a spot in their garage where I could keep my bikes, too. Sometimes Mr. Rouse would oil the chains for me, tighten the wheels and seats, and clean them up.

Summers gave way to shortened days and cooler nights. I longed for winters to be over so I could once again open my window that faced their house. From the time that spring would finally get here, all through the summer, and into early fall, I would have my window open, anticipating late afternoon when Mr. Rouse would come outside, walk around from his back porch and with a loud metallic screech, open the basement door.

As the day started its methodical ritual of completion, another type of day would begin. I would feel and see the dusk take over its time, as I saw the sun go down behind the roof of their house. The shadows would mark their time with their descent down our house and across the Rouse's yard. I took all that in as I sat right there at the window, eager with anticipation that as soon as Mr. Rouse reached that last stair, the next act would be for him to turn on a light. The first light of the night was not starlight overhead for me, but from earthbound fluorescent strips hung low over a workbench. As I watched I saw him move to the workbench, pick up a couple of things, put a pencil in his shirt pocket, walk then over to a shelf, remove a box, take a brown bottle out of it, pour a golden liquid into a small glass, drink the contents in one motion, set the glass down, put the bottle back, walk back to the work area, lift up an iron, look at it, look up out the window, and smile. Did he smile at me? I would have immediately ducked down. I don't think he ever saw me. He never called out anyway. I'd have stayed on the floor for a few moments, then slowly have risen up and looked over the sill. His head would be bent, as he looked at his tools or jars. While I hid, he would have turned on his radio, and then started his evening's work: Henry Mancini and Jack Rouse Duet for Vacuum Cleaner and Toaster Repair, Sonata #2.

I pulled my shade down to about two inches from the sill, changed into my pajamas, got my Nancy Drew, turned on my radio real low, read for a few minutes, then decided to go to the foot of my bed and watch Mr. Rouse work some more. I could sense everything about that workshop and once more I welcomed the aroma of the contents of that brown bottle, and then I fell asleep.

Funny thing was, on the nights that he worked, I didn't need newspaper or a bucket by my bed. I can't remember when I stopped needing them. I just know that sometime between when he started working in that basement and when my folks didn't need help anymore, I didn't get sick in the night. Something about repairing irons.

Clean Kill

I guess one could say that a football shot through the middle with an arrow would be considered a clean kill. Among my outside play toys as a kid, my football was my favorite thing to play with. It was brown leather with white stripes on each end. I didn't even have to throw it particularly to anyone. The field beside our house was large enough that I could kick it just about anywhere. I knew, even as a youngster that I wouldn't be able to reach the railroad tracks. But I liked to aim for them just the same. And, I could make some distance. Not bad for a girl.

Outside in that same field, my dad set up every summer his targets for practicing his bow shooting skills in anticipation of hunting season. He had a big round target with a multi-colored bull's eye. It was stuffed with straw and then propped on a big easel contraption. Depending on how one spread the legs, the angle of the target face could be adjusted. Dad used this target the most for practice. From time-to-time, he would stack up two or three square bales of hay and put assorted black and white targets on this prop to shoot against. Some of these targets were in the shape of deer and some were round.

He had a large bow that was unusual in shape. It was thick in the middle part where the left hand goes, and this part also was covered with leather. From both the top and bottom of this grip, the wood limbs would taper to an almost perfect "C" above and below. The wood quality was notable, too. The limbs were multi-laminated composites of maple, bamboo, and bubinga for strength and beauty. If one took that bow and set it upright on a table, it would have looked like a Texas longhorn steer rack. The wood was golden striped, and it was shined to a high gloss.

I remember when he brought the bow home to show Mom and me. He had just bought it and was very proud of the purchase. He went on to describe how it had been custom-fitted to him and how he had picked out the wood himself. Mom was not amused, but I thought the bow was pretty. The string was thick and so taut I couldn't pull it when Dad let me try. Those arrows had their own special quiver and I was not allowed to touch them. These were kept in a special place at our family store and I seldom ever saw them. He said this kept the string from getting brittle and breaking. He kept at least a dozen arrows in the dark brown leather quiver. The arrows were not his hunting arrows. He had a separate quiver for them and this he always kept at our family store. I was not allowed to touch them, and I seldom ever saw them.

These arrows for target practice had a short point that almost looked like the head of a bullet. They could easily penetrate a straw-backed target from about twenty feet away, and likely they could go through a human body, with that bow.

****

Dad had his picture taken with his first whitetail buck. He had been hunting with friends and on the signal of one of his buddies he fired his rifle and brought the deer down. According to what Dad told me later, in hunting talk it was a "clean kill." He was proud of that deer and he had it mounted by a taxidermist right away. We kept some of the meat that he had harvested in our freezer at home. One particular part was his favorite, the heart. In our stove,

Mom had a deep recessed pot, a built-in forerunner to the modern crockpot. She stewed that deer heart all day long so Dad could have it for dinner. I didn't much care for it, but I liked the other parts okay. Mom preferred the steak cuts so she would set aside those for us, leaving Dad to enjoy his heart all to himself.

The next deer that he killed was a doe and he did get that one with his custom bow. He didn't mention whether this was a "clean kill," and after that I don't recall that he used his bow for anything more than target practice.

He often went duck hunting and he always brought these back to the house to be cleaned for us to eat later. He got these using a shotgun so we had to watch out from time to time for the occasional spent shot that was missed in cleaning. I loved roasted duck and we had that frequently. The only ones that we didn't eat were the ones that Dad kept out to be mounted for his collection. He had a representative of all the common wildfowl types in our area: mallard (drake and hen), black duck, pintail, redhead, merganser, bufflehead, blue-winged teal, green-winged teal, wigeon, goldeneye, and a coot.

Dad placed these mounted animals along with his mounted bobcat all around the store, with some of the birds on the top shelves. In the front of the store, on top of the display windows inside, there was a large storage area and that's where he kept the mounted doe and bobcat.

Most people didn't even know they were up there unless Dad pointed them out. Along one of the walls, he placed some mounted mourning doves captured in escape flight with a framed mural of woods and water in the background. That same background showed up in some of his pictures of people, too. On the shelves in our store the mounted wildfowl kept company with squirrels. There were no rabbits or other small mammals. Maybe these didn't particularly interest him. While he had a lot of ducks, he did have two hawks in the mix. One was a red-tailed hawk and the other was a sparrow hawk. Dad said he had found them dead on the ground while hunting, but they were mounted with wings spread and poised as if seeking prey. Years later I had taken the stuffed sparrow hawk to live with me where it remained until it finally crumbled into sawdust and feathers.

He took his rewards of hunting to a taxidermist in a nearby town, and I often accompanied him on those trips. In the case of the deer, he cleaned and gutted the carcasses and wrapped them in canvas for the trip. Once there, he would discuss mounting options with the owner while I looked around the store. The shop had a huge display of animals in various mounted poses and several stacks of hides on the floor. On one visit, the owner gave me a hide as a gift. While I liked the hide very much, I was curious about the couple of holes that could be seen on the underside. I knew they were bullet holes, but my curiosity focused on the story that those holes would have told if they had talked. I wondered if the occupant of that hide had experienced a "clean kill."

What interested me was that none of Dad's mounted animals ever made an appearance at our house. My mother was not a fan of hunting and she probably tolerated his passion at that time for it. One compromise for certain was that there was not one mounted bird or fish or anything like that in our den or even in his bedroom. The house was occupied solely by the living.

****

On the occasion of the great football demise, when Dad came home from our store, I saw him gather up his bow and arrows from the back of his pickup truck and walk over to practice in the side yard. I wondered which of the targets he would use that day. I put on my shoes and socks and decided to go out and watch from the picnic table. Mom had shouted out the back door for us not to take too long as she was getting supper ready. As I walked out the back door, I heard the bow string sing out the release of tension and arrow; and then I heard this thump and a swoosh sound. Looking toward what I thought was the arrow's path, I saw my football, flat and impaled. Definitely killed. It was a sad, sorry kind of a sight, and as I looked at my dad, all I could think to say was, "I guess you're going to have that damned thing mounted, too."

Dad couldn't think of anything to respond, but he turned around and went back to his truck and got in. I stormed back into the house and Mom looked at me and asked where Dad was. I pointed out the window to the truck, and she went out the back door and over to him. A few minutes later she came in, with the football corpse in hand. The arrow had been removed leaving just the hole in the side.

"What do you say, let's go into town tomorrow morning, and see what's on sale at the Western Auto," Mom suggested. "You might find something in there that you like, and then we'll go next door to the drug store and have lunch....Dad's treat."

Brenda Lee Saved Christmas in Elkton

" 'Twas the night before Christmas, and all through the town, not a creature was buying, holiday sales were down." Such was the mood for Robinson's Department Store during the holidays in 1962. Mom and Dad were particularly glum as they had brought in a substantial amount of new inventory. The clerks had stocked the shelves, but the shelves were remaining full. Dad remained optimistic, but the number of days was shrinking before Christmas Day, and the prospects were slim. He would have to think of something clever to bring in customers if he was going to turn things around.

****

When Dad took over the family store, a few years after his Navy tour ended and the boondoggle that was Sun Valley was finished, he brought few skills to the business. Sure, he could talk and he had a way with people, but a head for retail business was not his. In a hurry, he needed to acquire some business sense to make the store succeed. His father, Harry Robinson, had been very successful at the business. He had built up a clientele over the years; and if his wife's parents could have seen how Harry prospered they would have congratulated themselves again and again for making such a successful match between Harry and their daughter, Sadye. The store had been her dowry for the arranged marriage and the importance of that attachment was not lost on Harry for one moment. Originally named Millers, Harry changed the name to Harry Robinson's Department Store. He built the business on his hard work and keen sense of knowing what the customer wanted. He was good with numbers and kept immaculate records. One of Harry and Sadye's daughters, Margaret, inherited this same ability for figures and keeping records, but ultimately she was not the one to take over the store. When Dad first came back from the Navy he had no interest in running the store, so he bought a nearby tavern and park, renamed it Hobby's Sun Valley and proceeded to lose his shirt.

After the end of that enterprise, he returned to the store and took over the entire operation from his sister. His father and natural mother had died, and while Dad had to jump through some legal complications with his father's widowed second wife, he ultimately prevailed and the store was his. He decided to specialize in Sunday-best clothes and shoes for men and women, work and hunting boots, and work jeans and jackets. He supplemented this with budget and better qualities of undergarments for men and children. He added a second floor retail level that was devoted to women's clothing and foundations.

He converted a small room in the back of the second floor where women's hats were displayed. Prior to remodeling this section, the second floor had been the apartment lived in by his parents. Their living room faced the main street with two large windows, and a third window faced the alley leading to the street. Now the occupants were ladies dresses, hosiery, and girdles. Mom and Aunt Margaret were in charge of this floor leaving Dad, Ernie, Betty, Anna Lee, Hilda, Jewel, Ruby, and Marion to work the downstairs and only fill-in on the second floor when needed. During the store's lifetime all of these women worked either part-time or full-time and were as much a part of the store as my parents.

Marion and Hilda were especially adept at keeping the downstairs inventory rotated and looking fresh. Dad didn't really pay attention to display quality, and didn't see the necessity of dusting and arranging. However, it was always obvious that the place looked the best when the ladies were involved with the care. The heavy lifting for Dad was talking to customers and fitting the men with shoes or jackets. He kept his camera in front near the cash register just in case a photo opportunity presented itself.

When various seasons came around, the store display windows were changed to note this timing. For instance, in September he and Ernie changed out any summer remains to showcase the fall hunting season and back-to-school. Since he had two windows, he used each for different themes. Generally, the hunting and similar themes were directed more to the men and were in the left-facing window. The other window featured women's wear and shoes, which Mom and the other women prepared.

It was great fun helping Dad with his side as this meant a field trip away from the store. We would go to the woods, rake canvas bags of leaves, gather downed branches, and even pick a bushel of "chinky pins." The correct spelling of that delicious nut is chinquapin, but I doubt if few knew that or cared for that matter. We considered ourselves very lucky if we came upon one of those big bushes. All I knew was that when we came back from our outing, we were more excited about getting that nut than anything brought back for the windows.

****

In the days of small town department stores, the best advertisement was what was displayed in those windows. Most of the traffic in these towns, before shopping malls, was along streets with the retail businesses lined up beside restaurants, furniture stores, five-and-dime stores, grocery stores, and drug stores. When customers came into town from the outskirts or from the countryside, particularly on Saturdays, they could be expected to frequent all the establishments they saw on one trip. With purchases loaded into cars or wagons, they returned to their homes or farms until they repeated the cycle the next week. While Dad advertised in the local paper and sent out flyers on occasion, he relied on the local residents to come by and see what he had in the way of new clothing or shoes.

In late summer there was a big rush to get children ready for school, and shoes topped the list of purchases. I helped out on Saturdays then since the business was that good. I often saw a number of kids I went to school with, so this was a great social event for me as well. There were a couple of families I looked forward to seeing each week. One family had a teenage daughter my age and we would talk while the family shopped. Her youngest brother had the whitest hair of anyone around and it stood out grandly amongst his dark-haired siblings. In contrast to this white and dark, we had another family in which every single member was a brilliant orange redhead. The mom, the dad, and all the kids had the exact same color hair and when they came in the store, it was if a big wall of flame swallowed all the merchandise as they moved down the aisles toward the blue jeans.

As fall moved toward the holidays, Dad shifted the store inventory around to create new exposure for cooler weather options. The red plaid hunting jackets displaced the seersucker sport coats and the corduroy pants displaced the lighter cotton ones. The dress boots were arranged in front of the shoes and the hunting boots had a counter all their own. Upstairs, women's sweaters came out of storage and replaced blouses. Wool skirts took over the dress racks. Sometimes there would be limited promotional items, not related to clothing, that would be stocked. I remember things like big thick coloring books and jewelry boxes and even sleds. Anything that enticed a customer to buy was considered a part of the effort to gain business.

In 1962 the climate of the country was somewhat unsettled, and this undercurrent of fear of the Russians and concerns of the economy did not go unnoticed or unfelt in Elkton. While the new young President was hailed as a great icon of change, rural America was still struggling with old ways. It was clear that the economy would change and that purchasing trends of the consumer were about to undergo a significant transformation. We saw the introduction of the color television with more channels available. We saw the introduction of transistors and this initiated portability of electronics. There was more exposure to plastics and this was destined to revolutionize everything, especially the automobile.

While these things were going on all around Elkton, my dad's immediate worry with the holidays just around the corner was whether he was going to sell the entire additional inventory he had brought in. This particular year he had purchased heavy and he sure didn't want to be stuck with overstock. He extended extra credit to customers if it meant they would buy just one more pair of *something*.

Some of his concern overflowed into our household and there was a cloud of dread hanging like dull ornaments on a worn-out tree. Both Mom and Dad were working harder than ever but ideas were just not rising to the surface. In their desperation to remain positive, they fell into frequent traps of sniping at one another, usually over simple things.

On the one particular day when I left for Harrisonburg to visit with some friends and do a little shopping, I was not feeling too good about how the holidays were going to pan out for us. My escape for a few hours was all that I could do in light of everything. There was a forecast for snow and I thought that if the prediction was right, then maybe customers would need boots and outerwear.

That evening when I returned, it wasn't late, but it was already dark and the snow had developed into a nice steady fall. There was no accumulation yet, but it was at least sticking. As I crossed over the river bridge at the edge of town, I saw the brightly lit town decorations. The holiday spirit was apparent as I approached the railroad tracks which crossed right in the middle of town. I heard something that sounded like singing, rolled down my window and was met with a woman's voice coming through a loudspeaker. I tried to locate its origin as I drove into town, and soon realized that it was coming from our store. In fact, it was blaring right through the upstairs windows onto the street.

Then, I saw Dad on the sidewalk standing by Mom and the rest of our crew. There they were right in the middle of falling snow! They were laughing and speaking to other townspeople who had gathered. When I parked and got out I realized that it was Brenda Lee singing, "Rockin' Around the Christmas Tree;" and its happy tune had infected everyone within earshot.

I asked Dad what was going on. He shared that earlier that day he decided that what was needed was something to liven up the town. He hooked up our old record player to a couple of cast-off car radio speakers; and he brought over from the house all our Christmas albums. He said that once he started playing those records, customers gravitated to the store and just about everyone who came in left with something they had purchased. I had already missed Johnny Mathis and Elvis Presley, who created a run on blue jeans. Dad was convinced that as customers browsed around they whistled or hummed whatever they heard and this put them in a better frame of mind to buy. Who could resist not having a happy holiday when coaxed by the likes of Brenda Lee?

For the remainder of the evening up until closing time, and for the next couple of days until Christmas Day, Dad played all those records, but he particularly played Brenda Lee the most. In subsequent years, he hooked up the record player and played them all until finally the records themselves just wore out.

For the longest time, Dad was convinced that Brenda Lee saved our store and our Christmas that one year. Here was the best line in the song: "You will get a sentimental feelin' when you hear, Voices singin' let's be jolly, deck the halls with boughs of holly." The sentiment overflowed from the store to the house and back into town that year. The snow continued to fall, and accumulate; customers came in by the dozens to buy warm clothes, boots, thermal underwear, and wool socks.

Dad treated Mom to a new Pendleton wool suit and I got a new record player with remote speakers. Mom gave Dad a battery-operated Bakelite calculator.

The Old Home Place

Dad looked one more time at the house, empty inside, all the furniture gone, then he turned and walked down the front stairs, across the sidewalk and to his car. When he got in, he looked back, and for some reason, the image of Jessie holding Tangerine, their beloved orange cat, came across his line of sight.

He hadn't thought of that cat for over forty years and now it was right there. He remembered, too, how Jessie looked

142

with the cat. Her remarkable black, long wavy hair rose up from her high, smooth forehead; and this hair and Tangerine's fur were the most sensational attractions in their contrasts of textures and colors. Then as quickly as the visions had appeared, they were gone, and he felt an emptiness that seemed to go all the way back to the beginning of time. Where had that time gone?

****

When they first courted, Hobby showed pictures of his family home to Jessie. He sent some in the mail to her with a note that asked, "What do you think of the old homestead?" The Robinson family home was a large two-story brick home on the corner of two streets just across the creek from town. Partially blocked by this house was another two story house, but this one was wood with a metal roof. It had been painted white with the roof painted a deep forest green.

What Hobby didn't know at the time was that his parents, Harry and Sadye, had planned to give him that white house when he married. They were excited that he was seeing someone and that it seemed serious. That she was not Jewish didn't matter. Several of their family had married outside their faith as they settled into new lives in America. What mattered to them was his starting a family. Their daughters were married and Lillian had already given birth to a daughter. Margaret was still practicing.

When Hobby and Jessie married, his parents were delighted with their new daughter-in-law. Jessie spent much time with Sadye and learned to cook a number of Jewish dishes that were Hobby's favorites. She learned to clerk in the store as well so she could work side-by-side with Hobby. When he left to join the Navy, Jessie stayed on at the store and in the house, until she could join him. She had bought some furniture and the Robinsons gave her some things from their house, too. One of the prized possessions was their bedroom set. It consisted of a double bed, dresser, and night stand. Made of mahogany and in the style of Chinese Chippendale, Jessie learned that this had been a wedding present to Sadye from Harry. Hobby and his sisters were conceived in that bed, and in a few years, Hobby and Jessie would conceive their only child, me, in that bed.

****

The house underwent some transformation during the forty-two years that they lived there. However, this was nothing compared to the transformation of the couple that occupied it. As they added a room to one side which became the den, complete with fireplace, and linoleum floor, their own relationship had changed by additions and subtractions. A child was added, a busted business subtracted.

Long before the den was added, they added a bathroom of sorts downstairs. When I was born, they bathed me in the warmest room in the house, in the deep, large enamel sink in the kitchen. Mom didn't want to keep running up and down the stairs to the only other bathroom they had, so a toilet was installed in the pantry. As I grew, the pantry became even more fascinating because there were shelves along one wall that went all the way from the floor to the ceiling, some ten feet or so. They were about six feet in width and all-in-all there were probably a good twelve shelves.

On one particular shelf was a stack of orange ceramic platters that must have numbered about fifty or so. There were smoked glass iced tea glasses and plates that were blue and green. These were ceramic, too. Mom told me that they were Fiestaware, but I didn't know what that meant. I just thought they were pretty and didn't understand why we didn't use them. There were bowls, implements, all sorts of cooking pots, trays, books, and boxes with whatever inside that even Mom didn't know what they contained. No one seemed to talk about all the dishes and stuff in there.

In the wintertime between Thanksgiving and Christmas, the pantry, since it was not directly heated, was cooler than the rest of the house. Mom would put her holiday baked goods in there and the toilet lid made a convenient seat to sample the cookies and cakes. Dad liked to go in there a lot during that time of year. So did our friends and cousins. Dad's favorite baked goods were the Danish Wedding Cookies. Mom always made at least two fruitcakes, one with bourbon and one without. It seemed that after Christmas she always had to throw away the one without.

In the basement which could be reached by stairs from this same pantry Dad kept his worm farm. This farm consisted of an old two-sided enamel sink on legs. The basins were filled with dirt and kept moist. The worms or night crawlers lived in both sides and Dad would tend to it, moving worms from one side to another when they got to a certain size. On a shelf over the sink he had stacks of old coffee cans which he used to hold the worms he took when he fished. He fed the worms scraps from the kitchen and he was proud that his worms were quite large. Sometimes he let me play with the worms when he was down there or he allowed me to sprinkle the dirt with water. To keep the worms from dying, it was important that the dirt not dry out.

****

Dad didn't really have a favorite room in the house and when he and Mom no longer slept together, their bedroom became hers alone. Mom took this front room and purchased two twin beds and a chest of drawers. She had a closet built in one corner and she moved a rocking chair to rest near the warm air vent.

The wonderful bedroom set that had been given to them by his parents became Dad's bedroom furniture. Sometimes when he went away overnight to fish or on trips for the store, I was allowed to take naps in there.

Since this room was on the east side of the house, it got the morning sun and was spared the afternoon glare. It was the darkest bedroom in the house.

Several kinds of mysteries surrounded that old farmhouse. One was the hidden door to the attic. On the second floor just beyond the landing, next to the large hall window, there was a closet. This held mostly Mom's things, such as her beaver fur coat and her special Hudson Bay blanket jacket that Dad had gotten for her when they were first married. At the back of the closet on the left side was a hidden door and this led up to the attic. Dad's Navy leftovers were on the stairs. The biggest leftover was his Navy duffle bag and it was a treasure for me with its white and dark Navy wool uniforms. There were belts, caps, and insignia arm patches as well. I loved to take out the shirts and wear them around the house. I would also take the patches and line them up on the landing floor, white and black ones across from the Navy blue and red ones, my little imaginary battle field.

Another mystery revolved around something hidden in the newel at the end of the banister on the stairs where it met the landing at the living room floor. Dad came home one day convinced that someone had hidden a fortune in that large wooden structure. He had overheard a conversation that involved my mother, and his immediate assumption was that there was a conspiracy to hide some money. He got some tools from the pantry and set about to dismantle the piece. I pulled up a chair to watch. After a few minutes of prying and hammering, he realized that this was way too difficult to get into and that it was likely that no one had ever disassembled and reassembled this before. He gave up the search, put up the tools, and drove back to the store. Nothing was ever said about that adventure again. Mom had a carpenter come in and do some minor restoration and some painting. While we knew the newel looked a little different, anyone coming to the house couldn't tell that there had been a repair.

Years later, after college, when I got my first apartment, Dad gave me his bedroom set and bought himself another bed and dresser. I still have that bedroom suit with me and it resides in a room with its other acquired matching pieces: the old store cash register and the curved glass side-by-side cabinet he had kept in the back of the store. He stored his guns, cleaning materials and ammo in that cabinet, while I chose to fill it with mementos of travels and childhood. The bedroom suit, the cash register, and the cabinet are infused with mementoes of past lives; the fragrances and bits of store flotsam and jetsam of long ago remain trapped in compartments, drawers, and on shelves, only liberated from time to time. I call that bedroom "The Elkton Room."

****

Dad found it increasingly harder and harder to climb the stairs to his bedroom as the years moved on in their old house. His emphysema had worsened, and what neither knew at the time, he was harboring in one lung the infancy of a cancerous lesion.

Mom didn't like the upkeep of the big house, either. It was drafty in winter and in the summer the only relief from the heat was in the den with its window air conditioner. There was a television in there, but they both found it awkward and strange to watch any shows together. Mom preferred to watch her small black-and-white propped on the washing machine in the kitchen. But the whole house was just too much for her, and Dad couldn't quite bring himself to admit that it was too much for him. The inevitable was bound to happen, and when Mom announced one day that she wanted to sell the house and move to a smaller one, he had no choice but to accept.

What did he think of his old home place now? He had some decisions to make. What furniture did he want to keep? Mom had found a house up on Spotswood and it was significantly smaller and much of their furniture would have to go, but she didn't mind that. She wanted a smaller place that she could manage all on one level. To her delight the house was close to the drugstore she frequented and the post office so that she could walk to both easily.

Dad told Mom that he wanted to keep his bed and dresser, the green recliner, and his Lowry organ. Those were the only possessions there he laid any claim to. The rest of everything was hers and she sold all that was not needed in an auction. All of the Fiestaware, except for a couple of pieces, was sold. All the frosted glasses, all the other platters and boxes of restaurant remnants (contents still unknown) were sold. The last little bits of Sun Valley gone now for the final time.

The well-used and moth damaged Navy duffle bag didn't survive and must have been discarded as it never reappeared in the new location. So long to the Navy days. I'm not sure much was left in it anyway and the pictures were a much better record.

Dad continued to live at two places, the store and the new home. This habit was too entrenched to break, and the store was the only consistency for him. His old home place next door to his parents' old home place was gone and he would have a new place across town. The cord of history and emotion was severed.

He hoped that Mom had not forgotten to include the sheet music that went with his Lowry organ. He had no idea what to expect. Seemed like his life had taken many different turns, some of which he created himself, some of which just happened around him.

Maybe he would play his favorite song, "Just a Song at Twilight," at the new place.

The Little House on Spotswood

When Jessie decided what furniture would be moved to the new place and what would have to be sold, she didn't ask Hobby if he had an opinion one way or another. Even though she knew that the move was the best thing for both of them, she accepted that he had distanced himself from the entire transaction. He considered the new house to be hers; and he let her sell the old home place and make any decision that she wanted. He knew that long ago he had given up the rights to call any of the shots.

During their last separation he lived on the second floor of the store and that was not a pleasant experience. When they agreed to reconcile again, he conceded that he would go along with anything she decided. Jessie knew that Hobby could no longer go up and down stairs without getting extremely winded. And the home place was too much to care for after I, their daughter, left years ago for college.

The cottage she found was on a main street in town within walking distance of the drug store, post office, and even their store. This was perfect. She picked what furniture and other stuff she would take and what she would sell.

She sold the big dining room suit and most of the living room furniture. She held back Hobby's old green chair that he sat in to watch television and work his acrostic puzzles. She kept some of the end tables, and she kept the Lowry organ she had bought years ago for him. Hobby didn't play it much anymore, and when he did it was the same damn song, "Just a Song at Twilight."

She sold the kitchen furniture and everything that was in the pantry. While she kept a couple of the Fiestaware dishes, she was happy to get rid of the last remnants of the Sun Valley tavern days. There was no reason for her to dwell on that past. With the money she made from two yard sales, she bought some new furniture for the dining room, a new sofa, and new appliances for the kitchen. She had her twin beds and her beloved cedar chests and pie safe. She also kept her curved glass china cabinet. There were many objects in that cabinet that were special to her, not the least of which was a red and white cut glass cup with her name inscribed on it. There was a gravy boat that had been her mother's and there were color pictures of her and Hobby taken by a lake in small wooden frames.

She knew just how she would place the furniture at the new house. The pie safe and heavy linen chest went in the dining room with the new table and chairs that she had bought. Her twin beds and dresser went into the larger of the two back bedrooms. Hobby would get the back bedroom that was closest to the one bathroom. The big console television would go into the small room between the living room and her bedroom; and she thought that this could be where Hobby could watch his shows at night. She would be content to watch her own shows in the living room on her small portable television. She would leave his old recliner in the living room along with the love seat. She planned that Hobby would prefer the chair in the TV room, but she left it that once Hobby got to the house, he could decide just where he wanted it positioned.

On the porch she put up a card table with a cloth over it and some folding chairs. Against one row of windows she put the old hide-a-bed sofa she kept. She had plenty of space in the kitchen to store the pots and pans and dishes. While the space was sufficient, she didn't dare buy anything else. From the kitchen there were stairs to a spacious floored attic. She hauled up extra clothes and some boxes of unsorted stuff, like her sewing and knitting extras. Her paper goods were stacked on the stairs close to the door. She put some framed mirrors up on a couple of walls and then she added pictures of me and prints of pictures that I had framed and given them in the hallways. And, with that, she nested.

****

Hobby drove away and didn't look back. There was nothing left to see. His old home was gone; most of the furniture had been sold, even though she swore that she had saved his favorites. He had distanced himself from the whole process so he had no idea what was left. As far as he was concerned nothing was left for him. He drove the dreaded two miles up through town to the new address. He pulled up in front of the cottage. It was so small compared to the other home. It was white, and the shutters were shiny black. He noticed that the house had been newly painted as he detected the smell of some paint thinner hanging around. As he got out of the car and started up the walk, he saw that Jessie had planted marigolds and daisies in front of the boxwoods along the front of the house. In the morning light they became guide marks to the door. I can't do this he thought. I am just too old for change.

She had put a fragrant herbal wreath in the middle of the door just above one of the small panes and the red and green colors caught his eye. They would have to be his favorite colors. He wasn't going to rush; and he fought hard to keep back any hope of a smile. As he opened the door, he saw right away just across the living room his favorite old recliner. It was dark green naugahyde and the seat had a couple of splits in it that were covered by an old green chenille blanket. The faded and worn arms seemed to raise up and say, "Come over and have a seat." He didn't want to like this, but then again that was his favorite comfortable chair. As he sat, the sturdy old chair friend let out a familiar settling sigh, "Welcome home".

****

I had learned all this from my mom and my dad who told me about the house changes in their own separate phone calls. Dad's version was that he didn't want to stay sleeping at the store and he and Mom had reached an agreement as to how they would spend the rest of their lives. He would manage to like the little house and he knew that he would spend most of his time at the store. Dad feared that a divorce would be expensive and he would not recover from the consequences. Mom reconciled herself to the truth that she would not live with me. We just didn't get along all that well. She tried to understand, and she did accept that decision. Her consolation was to have a new house and make the best of her life with Dad. She laid down some rules, such as what groceries she bought for him and what laundry she would do. She did the linens, but he had to send his clothes out to be cleaned or laundered. She refused to watch "Mash" or "Benny Hill" re-runs, too. She could come and go as she pleased, and so could he. They would keep up the pretense of a married couple, but their reality was they lived together for convenience. So they believed.

One year during a massive heat wave I offered to put central air conditioning in the house. They couldn't agree on this since the system would only have one thermostat. The compromise was to install window units in their individual bedrooms, a unit in the TV room, and a unit in the living room, sufficient to cool the dining room and kitchen. On visits home, I watched in wonder as the two of them compared temperature settings and then went off to their units to make an adjustment. It was this way with the televisions, too. Back and forth my father would go from the little TV room to the living room to find out what Mom was watching. She contented herself to remain seated with her own entertainment.

It was difficult for me to find neutral territory when I visited, but I mostly ended up in the TV room with Dad. I, too, got up on occasion and asked Mom what she was watching. There were three activities that she did while she watched TV: She played solitaire Boggle, she knitted, or she worked crossword puzzles. When I interrupted her, she would issue an invitation to play cards or some competitive game. Unlike how it had been for me as a child, I was terrible at competing against her so I often declined.

In every drawer in every end table in the living room there was at least one pack of cards. She could set up "Spite and Malice," or Canasta or a Poker game in less than a minute, including shuffling. She kept a small change purse in one of the drawers that was filled with quarters, dimes, and nickels.

When I agreed to play one hand, and no more, she would move us into the dining room and lay out the table. The tiny kitchen was close enough that she could access Cokes and snacks with little effort. After a hand or two of

whatever, Dad would come in to the living room and he would see that we were not watching TV. Seeing us set up in the dining room, he would ask what we were playing, but he never asked who was winning. He'd watch for a few minutes, and then go back to his TV show. As he settled back into his chair, I could hear that familiar squeak of springs and creak of the wood frame.

I would lose another hand, another forty cents. Mom would ask if I wanted to play another hand. I didn't want to, but I did. And I would lose. And every time I visited, she would ask me to stay an extra night. I slept in her bedroom with her in one of the twin beds. The mattress springs were shot, but I didn't care. We both read for awhile. Just before turning out the lights, she would ask if the room temperature was comfortable enough, and we both would get up and look at the air conditioner unit's temperature setting. It was fine.

Love Always, Hobby and Jessie

All I have to do is write one true sentence about Hobby and Jessie, my parents. It must be the truest thing that I know: They met in a fever, the attraction was physical and when the fever broke they spent the rest of their lives trying to get well.

Hobby and Jessie came from about as contrasting a background as one would ever expect. While they both were born in rural Virginia, there any comparison stopped. He was the first generation son of a Lithuanian Jew father and a German Jew mother. He had two female siblings and several cousins and uncles living close by in the Shenandoah Valley. Hobby's parents had settled in Elkton and this was where he was born, too. His father received a department store as part of a dowry from his wife's family. Hobby grew up in this business, which was renamed Harry Robinson Department Store, and later known as Robinson's Department Store. An uncle in neighboring Luray, VA opened a clothing store as well, and this was known as The Big Robinson's Department Store.

Except for his Navy stint, Hobby had not lived anywhere else in his entire life. In fact, except for the houses he rented in the Navy, he had lived only in three other houses in his life, and all were in Elkton. The old homestead where he grew up, the house that was his wedding present from his parents, and the last house where he lived when he died were it.

****

Jessie was born to a Methodist minister and a homemaker mother. Her ancestral roots were Americana from places like West Virginia and North Carolina. Growing up, Jessie had nine other living siblings with her being the youngest daughter. She and her siblings had lived all over Virginia and North Carolina, part of the backup traveling team to a circuit minister. Jessie had been born in McGaheysville, VA, just five miles from Elkton, but she did not grow up in the area. Her father moved back to North Carolina to take over a church in Poplar Branch, and took his youngest children with him to re-settle.

Both Hobby and Jessie were born in the very early 1900's, yet Jessie was six years older than Hobby. Both had some college, but Hobby dropped out, returning home to help with the family business. Jessie completed the two year college program in foreign languages at Louisburg College. She had been married and divorced before she met Hobby; when she married him she was only twenty-seven. Hobby had not been married before, and he was only twenty-one when they married.

He loved hunting, fishing, photography and storytelling. She loved running, swimming, laughing, and parlor games. He loved to cook. She loved to eat. They both shared a love of the drink, for a while. They both liked people; and they wore their hearts on their sleeves.

They were both exceptionally good looking and snappy dressers. They made a striking and attractive couple. Hobby had his dark European serious appearance and demeanor. Jessie had her pale skin and lean athletic body which fit the current fashions of that time. Their senses of humor seemed to revolve around a mutual like of practical jokes; the ability to make each other laugh was a strong force in their compatibility. Most of the pictures taken of them early in their courtship and in the subsequent marriage show them either smiling, playing, or laughing with gusto.

****

It was not clear to me, and perhaps even to their friends and relatives, just when the intimacy of the marriage broke down. Some connection slipped and bouts of silence competed with words of anger for attention. The joy of having a child may not have been strong enough to keep the original love connection. Did my mother suffer from a post-partum malaise that she couldn't shake? Did my dad's wandering eye fail to stay still and focus solely on what was his? Were they not able to talk about any of this? Where was their sense of humor when it was needed the most?

The trials and convictions of their marriage bore the evidence of the extremes of strain. The mistrust of each one's words and actions; the ongoing separations and reconciliations were like a badminton birdie—back and forth, back and forth, sometimes over the net, but mostly caught in the netting. Accusations of deeds that belied guilt and innocence were not satisfactorily explained and therefore were left to their own interpretation. Some deeds had to be resolved using a payback that those outside of them would not have understood.

How could Dad explain that he had not attempted to set her car on fire by tampering with the wiring? Only when Mom took the car into the garage did she learn that a mechanic had left a work cloth on the engine from a previous service. How could Mom explain that she was not hiding money around the house in parts of the structure itself? Only when Dad failed in his attempt to dismantle part of the living room banister assembly did he learn that he was mistaken. During these episodes and all the other ones, they somehow failed to go back to the place where it began and what brought them together in the first place.

And just what was "it"? It had to have been the original attraction. Emotionally they moved on, but just to what did they move on? They spent years figuring out ways to leave only to see the plans collapse for one reason or another. At the end, they decided on their own refuges and this is what saved them together. Did they see friends leave or die and accept that maybe they were lucky to be alive? Did they look around one more time at what they could lose? Or did they consider what they would possibly even gain, if they could figure out a way to live out their remaining years together? Could they find a way just to be happy?

Dad's refuge was the store and his photography. Early on the store was Mom's refuge, too, but she broke away from it, whereas Dad could not. She had used the store as a place to catch up with her friends. Dad was a fixture in the store. He wasn't just bonded by inheritance and livelihood; he was fused to every part of the interior of that building. When I was still quite little, he started keeping many of his clothes and personal articles there. He had a bathroom with a shower; and he sent his laundry out to be cleaned. He had a cot in his office where he took afternoon naps. He even used one of his mounted deer to hold his clothes, belt secured by antlers. His fedora was caught on a daily basis by his red-tailed hawk as if it had been captured mid-flight as escaping prey.

****

His darkroom and photography supplies were on the second floor of the store and most evenings were spent processing his negatives and developing his pictures. He made a studio of sorts up there where he could take people to have their pictures taken or he could create little "photo picture lots," not unlike in concept to Hollywood film lots. Little stages imitated life in which he could pose people or in which he could pose his miniature alter ego doll and its squirrel companion. All of his published books came out of this studio and darkroom. His ability to create written descriptions for every one of his pictures was just short of phenomenal, and probably could never be repeated. From the time he was a youngster and all through his life, he had a remarkable sense for remembering even the slightest detail about someone or some event. That he remembered these and put them in his books is a gift.

His photography talent was so immense that one gets the sense that it was the camera that used Hobby to record the existence of Elkton and its inhabitants, not the other way around. In the capture of expressions of his human objects, the subtleties wouldn't be lost, as he caught just the right moment to push the shutter release.

What Hobby wanted most in life was to be loved. The only way he knew how to show this was in his pictures. That was the height of intimacy for him. He courted his subjects with an intensity that mimicked a real life courtship. In every picture he took, he captured the smallest part of himself, perhaps in the way the subject smiled or in the innocence of a child. The best way he knew how to make love was in the developing of his pictures. In the darkness of his developing room, he could sense just when the picture was ready. His caresses on the paper were tender and his observations were filled with a happiness and serenity that only he could define. This part of him could never be argued as the proof resided in the very pictures themselves. Pictures of all his friends. Pictures of everyone. Pictures of Jessie.

Hobby and Jessie loved each other, and, as my parents, I know they loved me, too. They loved their friends and family. They loved the Navy years and they loved their Elkton years. Despite their small attempts to leave each other, they knew deep inside that it would never happen.

They reconciled in the last fifteen or so of their years, and in this reconciliation they lived better together than they had in a very long time. They went dancing and ate out together at restaurants or at friends' homes. They accepted each other, and the pact they had worked. There were no more accusations and no more fights. They had achieved a peace; and then they grew old together, until the first one died.

****

Dad sold the store after Mom died and opened up a little store-front business, Hobby's Photo Memories, across the street from the original Robinson's. He had cameras and pictures on display along with his old store counters whose new job was to bear the weight of his photos, books, scraps of paper, and various odds-and-ends that accumulated. The fish head was nowhere to be seen, and I am not sure he remembered where it was. After he had died, I found it later in the back of the old store.

During his last couple of years, my dad no longer picked up his camera to take pictures. He seemed content to talk about picture taking more than actually taking the picture. His hands shook a little, and maybe this made him uncomfortable with the camera. While he had fully recovered from the cancer in his lung, his strength had been diminished. But that didn't stop him from telling his stories. He showed up at his cramped photo store every day, and waited patiently for anyone to come in. When people came in to have coffee, and to sit and talk with him, he eagerly told his stories and talked about his pictures. He often included some personal experience just to add the right amount of drama as background to the artist.

Such was the story of the notch in his left ear. From a past surgery, he had a "notch" left from an excision on his ear to remove a skin cancer. Even though he had options to cosmetically improve the appearance of that ear, he chose to keep the notch. He said it gave him character. After he died, and I was clearing out the store, some out-of-town visitors came in to look around. They had just learned that Hobby had died and wanted to see if there were some items that could be purchased. They bought some photos and books, but left me with a story that only my dad could have created. When they had asked Dad about the notch in his ear, he explained to them that he had experienced a close call with a bullet, and he was lucky that the damaged ear was the only after effect. I could not bring myself to deny that version. It was too good of a "Hobby story" and I decided that it should remain as part of the folklore. Maybe I should have added to their story by inserting my own version: that the incident of the close call happened at the infamous tavern, Sun Valley, VA, during its last night of operation.

My mom—Jessie—and my dad—Hobby—were buried side-by-side in the Elkton cemetery. This was a fitting location for them since I was as much determined to keep them together as they might have tried to split apart in years past. Dad had once said he wanted to be buried in

Harrisonburg, but there was never any doubt in me that he would ever leave Elkton. The invisible cord that bound both of them to this place was stronger than any natural force. They were bound by the connection of family and place, or perhaps it was the water.

While I inherited their genes for determination and stubbornness, along with their sense of humor, I know I inherited their love of Elkton as I returned to Virginia to live close by. Perhaps I have Virginia molecularly in my system. While I live about an hour's drive away, this is as close as their satellite can come.

****

They are resting now in the place that they both loved in life. The many chambers of their hearts were occupied by those they had met during their journeys from their births to their deaths. And still all the chambers were not likely filled. I know that there was a chamber in each of their hearts that no matter how badly it might have been broken still had room for even just a wee bit of love for each other. They got well and just didn't know it. They might not have been able to say the words, and maybe they didn't show their love in more conventional ways; but there was still some spark left.

My lasting memories of them are this:
Hobby, my dad, standing in front of the store, smiling, waving to passersby, shouting a greeting, glancing up and down the street. He has his camera just inside the door,

film loaded, ready to shoot. The right picture is just moments away.

Jessie, my mom, sitting at a table, decks of cards at the ready, smiling, asking if someone wants to play one more hand. Snacks prepared. Scorecard poised. Next deal just moments away.

Both of them at a VFW dance, a waltz has started; they take to the floor, gliding together in perfection of tempo and step, looking at each other. Mom's full skirt flows around capturing the music and keeps it close to their steps. Dad's hand rests gently on her back guiding at the right moment into a twirl that is flawless in its execution. The rest of the dance crowd has moved back, giving them space to perform the magic of their waltz steps. They are not even aware that they occupy the floor all by themselves.

Love Always, Hobby and Jessie

Love Always, Hobby and Jessie

Scenes from Where He is Resting Now:

Images from Hobby's Collection

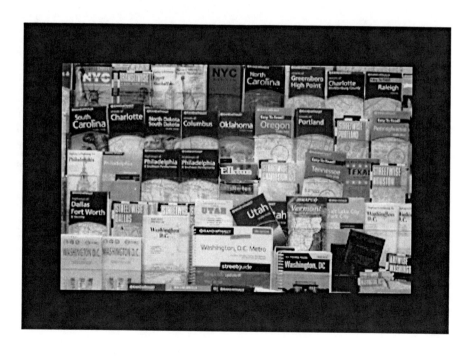

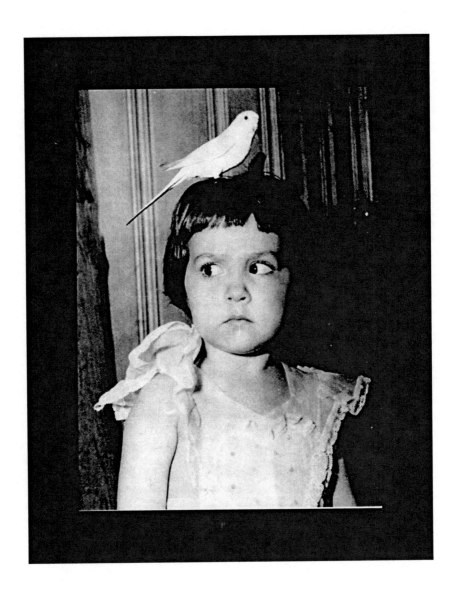

Author Bio

Recently retired from active working life, Sara Robinson has taken her prolific technical paper publishing and seminar presentations background, and turned this into an entire new direction. Previously a recognized global authority in the minerals processing and application industries, she now ventures into new realm for her—creative writing for pleasure.

This first work, her memoir of her parents, is the inaugural attempt with creative non-fiction. Her next projects include a murder-mystery series with the setting primarily in the Elkton, VA area and a collection of short stories.

Sara resides in Charlottesville, VA.

Breinigsville, PA USA
07 February 2010
232045BV00002B/2/P